Winnie and Lilly

Two Christmas Grouches

Celebrate Christmas

AF284309

1st Edition, 2020

Idea and Text:
© Daniela Landsberg, 2020

Editor:
Daniela Landsberg
c/o Familie Moltrecht
Zum Thelenkreuz 22
53859 Niederkassel-Mondorf

Title, Pictures and Coverdesign:
Dr. Rolf Peter Hampel-Landsberg, MD
Daniela Landsberg

Printing and publishing:
BoD - Books on Demand, Norderstedt

ISBN: 9783752625608

Bibliographic information from the German National
Library:
The German National Library lists this publication in the
German National Bibliography; detailed bibliographical
data are available on the Internet at http://dnb.d-nb.de.

Many thanks to Bianka and Ty Stumpf from Sanford, North Carolina, USA. With your painstaking help, both in the corrections and in the advice and suggestions, the story of Winnie and Lilly could appear in English.

Dear Readers,

First of all, thank you very much for purchasing my book. I hope that this Christmas story will give you and your family a little joy and put you in a Christmas mood.

My stories intentionally include topics that are not always happy but are still a reality. In this way, I would like to stimulate thought and offer a basis for discussion appropriate to the age of the child. It is also important to me that despite the serious issues, humor is not neglected. I also would like children to learn something positive from the stories.

It also is important for me to be largely neutral about the Christian faith in the stories because I think that it should be up to each parent to decide how he or she wants to raise children. That means that although I mention churches as buildings or nuns, I don't discuss them any further.

I wish you and your family a lot of fun reading, a nice holiday season, and a peaceful holiday!

Daniela Landsberg

"Again, this stupid Christmas!" Angry Lilly kicks the craft table. "Lilly, pull yourself together now!" Sister Maria warns her. "Pull yourself together? Do I look like a sheet of paper or what?" Lilly replies cheekily. "Lilly, that's it, go to your room and immediately!" Sister Maria points with her index finger towards the door. "Oh, what a shame! I would have loved to continue making these Emperor Nero wreaths," Lilly replies in a mock outraged voice. "These are Advent wreaths, Lilly, Advent wreaths. And you may no longer make handicrafts, but go to your room and think about your misbehavior," replies Sister Maria angrily. Lilly puts her right hand on the fir branches, "Sorry, Nero, but you have to get by without your wreaths now." Lilly pushes the fir branches over the edge of the table. These fall to the ground.

"Lilly!" shouts Sister Maria. "Stay calm, Penguin, I'm now going to my room to think about my misbehavior… maybe." With her tongue out, Lilly leaves the art room. "This child still drives me crazy." Exhausted, Sister Maria looks at the fir branches on the floor.

"Bovine spongiform encephalopathy comes from cattle and not from children," Lilly explains to sister Maria, who put her head into the door again. "Lilly!" Sister Maria shouts again. "Keep calm, Penguin, keep calm. I'm already gone." With these words, Lilly turns and slowly trots into her room.

At the same time…

"321, 322, 323, 324, 325, 326, 327, 328, three hundred twenty…" Santa Claus hesitates. He looks at Christmas Elf 327 and 329 alternately. "Sepp, Hugo, where's Winnie?" he asks the two Christmas elves. "So, Winnie…yes…," Sepp hesitates. "He didn't want to help," Hugo cut him off. "Why? Don't help?" asks Santa Claus indignantly. Hugo shrugs and raises his arms, "We tried to persuade him, but he just didn't want to." "He just didn't want…Such a thing doesn't exist at Santa Claus!" Angry Santa stalks off to look for Winnie.

"If you're happy and you know it, clap your hands
If you're happy and you know it, clap your hands

5

If you're happy and you know it
And you really want to show it
If you're happy and you know it, clap your…"
"Winnie! What are you doing there?" Santa Claus calls out in a loud voice. "Aaahhhhh!" Winnie is startled. Pink and light blue confetti flowers fly in a high arc through the from the bag Winnie was holding in his hand. Winnie looks innocently at the confetti pile that has landed at Santa's feet. "Great, thanks, Santa Claus, now I have to start again," Winnie says indignantly. "Start again?" Santa Claus doesn't seem to believe his ears, "What does it mean to start again? Nothing is going to start over here. You explain to me what's going on here!" Winnie looks around proudly in his room, "You see that, bad…um…dear Santa…I decorate." Santa Claus snorts angrily, "Winnie, does it look *Christmasy* in here as it should?" Winnie snorts playfully, "Does it look like your room? Or maybe like that of the other 1294 Christmas elves?" Winnie shakes his head,

6

"Nooooo, this looks like my room…and this is my room, too," he states energetically. To reinforce it, Winnie crosses his arms over his chest. "Winnie…it's *Christmas*…you are a *Christmas* Elf," Santa tries to explain in a calm but determined tone, "that means that you have to help with the preparations and decorate everything for Christmas." Winnie defiantly goes to his closet and pulls out another bag of confetti flowers. "But I don't like to have Christmas. I want to have spring!" With these words, he reaches into the bag with his right hand and throws a handful of confetti flowers into the air.

At the sight of the confetti flowers, which are slowly falling to the ground, Winnie's mood changes suddenly. "Whee…that's nice! Look, Santa Claus, how they fly!" Without words, Santa Claus leaves Winnie's room and goes into the large living room.

There he sits down in his large red armchair next to the fireplace. Immediately there are a dozen Christmas elves around him including Sepp and Hugo. Santa thinks for minutes, and in the meantime, scratches his beard. "It doesn't work anymore with Winnie like this," he finally says. "He behaves as if he were the spring god himself. No, it can't go on like this!" "But what do you want to do about it, dear Santa?" Hugo asks carefully. Santa Claus kneads the tip of his red nose. "That's a very good question, Hugo, a very good question," he replies thoughtfully. "I think I'll sleep on it for one night. I'm sure something will come to mind by dawn," says Santa firmly. Santa Claus claps his hands and then actively rubs them. "So, guys what do you have to report? What do the TV shows in the children's rooms?" Immediately the elves start talking wildly.

"So, there is a girl who has…"

"The little boy with the toy car…"

"The two siblings quarrel all day…"

"The girl from the children's home…"

"Stop! Stop! Stop! Not all at once," Santa Claus interrupts the elves. "I can't concentrate at all."

He looks at Elf 327. "Sepp, start it," Santa says. Sepp clears his throat for a moment and then starts to tell excitedly. "So, there is a little girl in the children's home. Her name is Lilly. And Lilly doesn't like Christmas at all. She doesn't really like anything. She's just cheeky all the time and doesn't listen to what the adults tell her." Santa and the other elves listen intently. After Sepp is finished,

Santa Claus looks around thoughtfully, "So, the girl doesn't like Christmas," says Santa Claus to himself. But Sepp nods immediately and confirms, "Yes, she doesn't like Christmas and just nothing," he repeats. "It's interesting, very interesting," says Santa Claus, still thoughtful. The elves look at each other questioningly.

"Why is that interesting, dear Santa? It's terrible if someone doesn't like Christmas," Jakob asks in surprise. Santa carefully strokes Elf 318 over the head, "You know, Jakob, maybe I have a good idea. But I'll tell you tomorrow. I have to clarify something first." The elves look again questioningly, but they know that if Santa wants to keep something to himself, he can do it quite well (unlike the little elves, who sometimes spill out of sheer excitement). "Well," says Santa Claus, "now the others, what can you tell me about the other children?" he asks with interest. The elves immediately begin to tell. After all the elves have told their stories to Santa, it is well after midnight. The first elves are already yawning. Some rub their little eyes. Santa Claus looks around. "So, you little elves, it's time to go to bed. Quickly into the bathroom. Brush your teeth and put on your pajamas. There will be a lot to do tomorrow." "Oh, I'm too tired to brush my teeth," Vincent lisped through the gap in his teeth. "But if you don't brush your teeth, the bad bacteria cause tooth decay," says Theodor knowingly. "Oh, no,"

Vincent replies defiantly and heads for the bathroom.

After all the elves have gotten ready and are lying in their beds, Santa Claus goes from room to room to wish everyone a good night. When he gets to Winnie's room, he hears a crooked song outside the door.

"Under the sea – Under the sea – Darling it's better – Down where it's wetter – Take it from me…"

"Winnie, you should sleep," Santa Claus interrupts Winnie's singing. "Aaahhhhh!" Winnie is startled again. Again the utensils are flying through the room in a high arc. This time it's a handful of brushes and a wide range of colors.

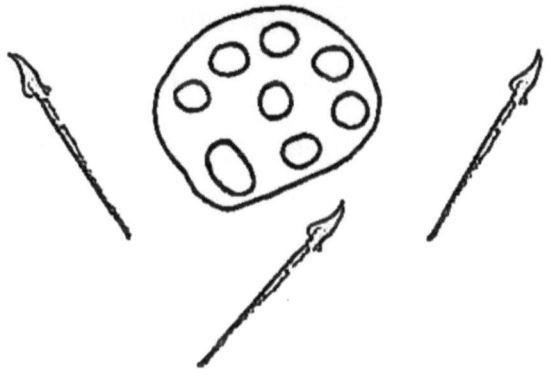

Winnie looks indignantly at Santa. "Thank you, Santa Claus! Now I can paint everything again." Winnie tears off the top sheet of his pad, which he had placed on his large easel. With a look at the smeared work of art, he sighs briefly, then picks up his painting utensils, and starts painting a beach landscape again. Without further attention to Santa Claus, Winnie starts singing again. This time a little louder and more crooked than before, "Under the sea – Under the sea – Darling it's better – Down where it's wetter – Take it from me..." Santa turns around speechless and continues his rounds. After closing the last door of the last elf, he goes to his room. He looks at the watch. "Hm, after 3:00 a.m.," he says. "Then I have to wait until morning," he says quietly to himself. After Santa Claus has also made himself ready for bed, he lies down and falls asleep immediately. Now it is almost completely quiet in the long hallway. Rustling, rumbling and rattling only come from one room. But at some point it is quiet in this room, and Winnie fell asleep.

Five hours later, Santa is sitting at his desk and rolling over the thick phone book that lies in front of him. "Children's home Sankt Katharina. Yes, that's it," says Santa Claus to himself. He picks up the phone and starts dialing the digits one by one on the large dial.

"Children's home Sankt Katharina, Sister Theresa here" announces the tender voice of the nun. "Good morning, Sister Theresa, this is Santa Claus speaking. Would you be kind enough to give me Sister Maria?" Santa asked politely. "Oh, dear Santa Claus. This is a surprise that you are calling us. I'll get Sister Maria on the phone right away. Please wait a moment." Before Santa can answer, Sister Theresa put the phone aside to get Sister Maria. Santa Claus is listening to the murmur of the elves in the hallway. "Good morning, this is Sister Maria speaking. Santa Claus?"

"Um, yes, good morning, Sister Maria," Santa Claus hesitates briefly. "How can I help you?" asks Sister Maria. "Is it about one of the children?"

Santa Claus nods. "Yes, exactly, about one of the children. I hear from the elves that a little girl named Lilly lives with you." "Oh, Lilly," Sister Maria interrupts Santa Claus. "What does that mean?" Santa Claus asks. "You know, dear Santa, Lilly is a very difficult child. She doesn't follow rules and boundaries, she's not interested in anything or anyone, and she doesn't care about anything," explains Sister Maria. "So? And then she probably doesn't like Christmas either?" asks Santa Claus. "Christmas? She hates Christmas," sighs Sister Maria. Santa strokes his long white beard, then says, "I have a little guy here, too. His name is Winnie. And somehow he likes everything else except Christmas." Sister Maria listens carefully. "I thought we could bring the two together. Maybe they can bring each other closer to Christmas," Santa Claus suggests. Sister Maria thinks for a moment, then asks, "How is that supposed to work?" Santa Claus also thinks about it. He admits, "Hm, maybe I can think of

16

something." Sister Maria speaks, briefly telling Santa Claus about her idea, and together they decide to put it into practice. At the end of the conversation, the two say goodbye to each other and agree to stay in touch. After hanging up the phone, Santa goes out to the hall to find Winnie in his room. From afar, he hears another song.

"The Winnie likes it colorful, the Winnie likes it colorful, the Wieienie, the Wieienie, the Winnie likes it colorful. The Winnie…" emerges from the room, sung to the tune of "The Farmer in the Dell."

"WINNIE!" Santa Claus interrupts him loudly. "Aaahhhhh!" Winnie is startled again. This time, a handful of Hawaiian flower chains fly across the room. One of them lands directly on Santa's head. When Winnie sees this, he starts to laugh out loud.

"You look funny, colorful Santa Claus," says Winnie cheerfully. "Winnie, it can't go on like this. I have to talk to you. Come with me to the meeting room!" Santa Claus directs Winnie. "What is it about?" asks Winnie as he picks up the Hawaii flower necklaces from the floor. "I'll explain that to you there," replies Santa Claus. When Winnie sees that Santa is already in the hallway, he runs after him.

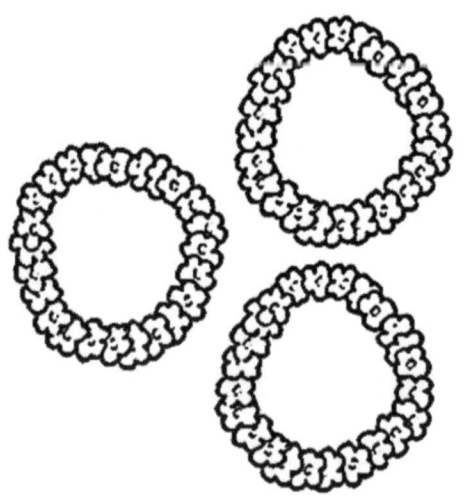

Once in the meeting room, Santa Claus sits down in his large armchair behind his desk. Winnie takes a seat in front of it in a chair. "Well, Winnie," Santa Claus begins the conversation, "I have the impression that you don't like Christmas at all…" "No, I much prefer spring and the sun and the mountains and the sea," Winnie interrupts Santa. "Winnie, you are an elf, a Christmas Elf. Your job is to help shape Christmas." Winnie shakes his head, "I don't like that at all. I much prefer to design spring and summer." He thinks for a moment. "The Easter bunnies are allowed to do something in spring. Why not me?" he asks defiantly. "Because you are not an Easter bunny," Santa Claus tries to explain. "I think that's stupid," Winnie still answered defiantly, crossing his arms. "Why can't I be an Easter bunny?" he demands. Santa looks at him in disbelief, "Because you're an elf and not a rabbit," he says. Winnie looks to the side, pouting. "Look, Winnie, I have a job for you," said Santa firmly. "So? What kind of job is that supposed to be?" Winnie inquires. "So, there is a child from the children's home…"

"A child?" Winnie interrupts Santa Claus again. "Yes, ok, a girl."

"A *girl*? What have I got to do with a girl please?" Winnie asks indignantly. Santa replies, "The girl doesn't like Christmas any more than you do."

"Good child."

"I want Winnie for you to go to the girl and put her on the right path," Santa explains. Winnie looks at Santa Claus with wide eyes, "Should I play babysitter for a girl?", he asks surprised and indignant at the same time. "Yes. I mean, you're perfect for that. You don't like Christmas either…," Santa says.

"And no girls," interrupted Winnie. "Besides, what is that supposed to be? The girl doesn't like Christmas. I don't like Christmas. Shall we stand around the Christmas tree afterwards, decorate it, and sing Christmas carols?" Winnie asks sarcastically. Santa Claus nods. "Yes, that's roughly how we imagine it."

"We?"

"Sister Maria and I," replies Santa Claus. Winnie thinks for a moment. "Who is Sister Maria?" he then asks. "Sister Maria is a nun from the children's home," Santa answers. "A penguin?! Seriously now? Should I go to a penguin who has no control over getting a girl to decorate the Christmas tree?" Winnie can hardly believe what he is hearing. "That's the plan," says Santa Claus. "Are you kidding me?!" Santa Claus shakes his head, "No, Winnie, that's really the plan." Winnie looks at Santa Claus for a long time, then he asks, "First, why should I do this? Second, what do I get from it? And third, why should the girl like Christmas?" Santa Claus thinks for a moment. "First of all, each of us has a job. You can prepare Christmas here with us, or you can take care of the girl. Secondly, you might like Christmas afterwards, and thirdly, everyone likes Christmas... actually... it's the festival of love. You know, the girl has a very hard time. Maybe you can make her start to like things. And what

21

time is better for this than Christmas?" explains Santa Claus. Winnie folds her arms again and looks around the room. Then he looks Santa Claus directly in the eyes, "So you're sending me away because I'm different from everyone else here?" he wants to know. Santa Claus shakes his head, "No, Winnie, it's not like that. Rather, it is a big task that I would like to give you there. You know, maybe all the Christmas preparations are really not for you. Maybe you are destined for something completely different…"

"Sure, babysitting for little girls," says Winnie defiantly.

He hesitates a moment, then gets up. "Fine, then I'll go to the girl. But I'm not going to tell her to like Christmas. And I'm definitely not going to decorate a Christmas tree, sing Christmas carols, or bake cookies. Because that's girl stuff." With these words, Winnie leaves the meeting room and angrily stomps into his room.

There he takes his little suitcase out of the closet and starts packing his clothes. "Just send little Winnie away. Just because he's different from the others. It's so mean and unfair!" Winnie says angrily to himself. His gaze falls on the picture he painted in the night. He looks at the many colorful confetti flowers with which he has decorated his room. He strokes the Hawaiian flower chain, which he previously hung so lovingly over his self-made sun chair. "Maybe it's not too bad to go to the girl," he thinks. "If she doesn't like Christmas and I don't like Christmas, it can even be really funny," he says. Suddenly Winnie starts to smile, "Oh, and best of all, I don't have to do any Christmas preparations. It'll be great!" says Winnie. His bad mood has just vanished. In a good mood and in no time at all, he puts all his things in the suitcase that he wants to take with him.

"And you are coming, too," he says and grabs his little green swimming trunks. "Maybe the girl lives by the sea or elsewhere where there is water," he thinks. Winnie is so excited that he completely forgets that the girl lives also where there is now winter. When he has finished packing everything, he pulls his little suitcase out the door. Immediately all the elves gather around Winnie.

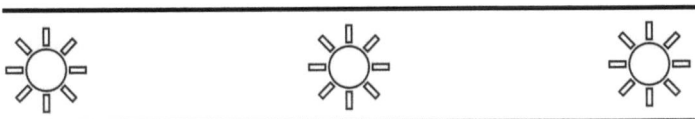

"Where are you going?" asks Sepp. "I'm on vacation while you are all allowed to work for Christmas," says Winnie. Santa Claus appears in the hallway before the others can say anything. "I've packed everything, Santa Claus. It's ready to go," Winnie calls out to him. "Well, that was quick," replies Santa Claus surprised. "Yes, yes, how do they say, don't waste any time." Santa nods. "That's right." He hesitates, "Did you think about it well?" he asks carefully. Winnie retorts, "And how I thought it over. I'm even looking forward to it." Sepp starts to cry, "But...but...when are you coming back, Winnie?" he wants to know. "Yes, exactly, when are you coming back?" Vincent whispers. Winnie shrugs. "I don't know that at all," he says. All elves look at Santa inquiringly. "You know, dear elves, Winnie will come back when he has mastered his big task ahead of him." The Christmas elves widen their eyes. "What task?" Sepp wonders curiously. "Winnie will go to the girl from the children's home and bring her closer to Christmas," replies the Santa Claus. "Winnie? Our Winnie should do that?" asks Jakob. "Yes, exactly, Winnie will take on this big task." Immediately all the elves start laughing. "Why are you laughing like that?" Winnie asks. "It's not strange," he adds. "Elves! Nobody laughs at another! Is that clear?!" Santa warned. Immediately all the elves are silent again. Vincent interjects, "May I ask something?" Santa Claus nods. "How is Winnie supposed to do that if he doesn't like Christmas himself?"

"That's exactly what it's all about, Vincent, that's Winnie's big job." The elves look at each other questioningly. "So, the difficulty is that, although

26

he doesn't like Christmas himself, Winnie is supposed to bring Christmas closer to the girl, who also doesn't like Christmas?" Theodor tries to summarize. "Right, Theodor, that's the way it is," Santa Claus confirms. The elves start whispering. "There is no whispering here," Santa Claus warns the elves again. "But we are afraid that Winnie will not make it," says Sepp and starts crying again. Theodor strokes his head. "Don't cry, Sepp, otherwise I have to start," Theodor tries to comfort Sepp.

Santa clears his throat, then walks up to Winnie, and puts his right hand on his left shoulder. He looks at the Christmas elves, then looks at Winnie. "Our Winnie will do it. I'm sure of it," he says with a calm and confident tone. After a brief moment, Sepp runs to Winnie and hugs him. "Take care, Winnie, I firmly believe in you! You'll do it!" he says and wipes the little tears from his face. All the other 1293 Christmas elves immediately arrive and hug Winnie. After everyone says goodbye to Winnie, Santa puts his right hand on Winnie's shoulder and looks at him thoughtfully. "Are you ready for your big job, Winnie?" Winnie nods. "Yes, I'm ready," he replies confidently. "Come on then, my little elf," says Santa Claus and claps his hands twice. And before Winnie knows, he's on his way to the orphanage to bring Christmas to a little girl.

When Winnie arrives at the orphanage, he looks around first. In front of him is a huge brick building with many colorfully decorated windows. He looks excitedly to the right and then to the left. He turns his head so far that he can almost look behind him. "There's no sea here or there," says Winnie, disappointed. At that moment the door opens in front of him.

"Hello, can I help you?" the nun asks kindly. "Yes, I'm Winnie, and I was sent here because the girl doesn't like Christmas," replies Winnie. "Oh, I also wish you a good day," he adds quickly. "So, you're Winnie. Come on in then. Santa has already told me a lot about you. I am Sister Maria, by the way," the nun replies gently. While Winnie runs alongside Sister Maria, he keeps looking right and left into the many rooms. "It's like ours," he notes. "We also have so many rooms."

"You are certainly one of a lot of elves then?" Sister Maria asks interested. "Yes, there are 1295 elves," Winnie replies cheerfully. "There are really a lot of you," smiles Sister Maria. "You're never bored then, are you?" Sister Marie comments. Winnie nods. "We are never bored," he agrees. "We always have something to do. Especially at Christmas time," says Winnie. "And you also have a lot to do?" Sister Maria would like to know. "Yes," replies Winnie, "I'm always very busy. I

30

paint colorful pictures, decorate my room, sing a lot, and do a lot of other great things in the best season of the year." "You mean Christmas time?" asks Sister Maria. Winnie looks at her in surprise. "But Christmas is not a season," he says firmly. "The seasons are spring, summer, autumn, and winter. And my favorite time of year is spring." Winnie is so happy with the thought of spring that his eyes start to shine. "But you're a Christmas Elf," notes Sister Maria. "Yes, that's right, but I'd rather be an Easter elf," Winnie replies wistfully. "Oh dear, it will be quite something then with Winnie and Lilly," thinks Sister Maria. "Now I'm going to show you your room first. You can already set up there. I'll pick you up in ten minutes and take you to Lilly. Okay?"

"Lilly. Yes, this is good," replies Winnie.

When he arrives in his room, Winnie puts his little suitcase on the bed and looks around. "A little dreary," he thinks, "no wonder there is no Christmas spirit here." "We'll have it right away," Winnie says aloud to himself and takes a few self-painted beach pictures and a bag of colorful flowers from his suitcase.

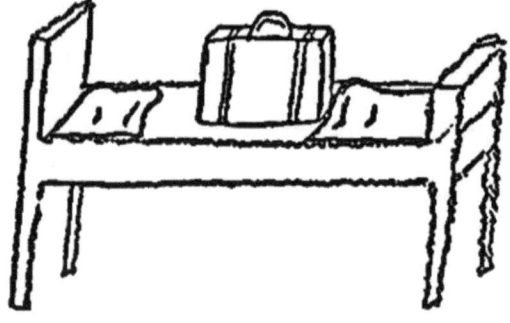

He immediately begins to sing again, "I have a dream — I hope it will come true — That you're here with me — And I am here with you — I wish that the earth, sea, and the sky up above – Will send me someone to lava…" Winnie is so eager and happy that he doesn't hear the knock on the door. He doesn't even notice the second knock. The door opens carefully. "Why they are all funny, nimble, and happily moving! Blackbird, Thrush, Finch, and Star and the whole flock of birds…" At that moment Winnie's gaze falls on Sister Maria, who is standing in the room with her mouth open. Winnie gently sticks another flower on the window without taking his eyes off Sister Maria. "Winnie, what are you doing?" Sister Maria wants to know. "I'm decorating," Winnie replies with a happy smile. Sister Maria looks around the room. "I see that," she then says, "but you already know that we have Christmas?" she asks, irritated. Winnie nods. "Yes, but of course, I know that." "Then why does it look like a holiday paradise to you?" Sister Maria asks. "Well, because I love the sea and the flowers," replies Winnie. Sister Maria grimaces, "Yes, that may be so, but it *is*

Christmas."

"And what does that mean?" Winnie asks defiantly. "Well, you can't decorate everything like in a holiday paradise. Everything has to look like Christmas," Sister Maria looks around again. "And to be honest, this doesn't look like Christmas," she says. "Good," says Winnie, sticking another flower to the window. "Winnie, listen, how are you going to bring Lilly closer to Christmas if you don't like Christmas yourself?" Winnie looks astonished. "Why does everyone say I don't like Christmas? I like Christmas," he says. "But there is nothing Christmas here. You have to decorate it for Christmas," tries to convince Sister Maria Winnie. "Who says that?" Asks Winnie. "Well, that's just part of it. Christmas is all decorated for Christmas and in spring and summer you can make a flower decoration." Winnie shakes his head, "No, no, you can do that now," he says, sticking another flower to the window. "I give it up," sighs Sister Maria. "Will you come with Lilly

34

now, please?!" she asks Winnie "Lilly, yes, of course," replies Winnie cheerfully and wants to get out of the door. "Please put the flowers away, Winnie," Sister Maria warns him. "But don't girls like flowers?" Winnie asks irritated. "But not for Christmas," replies Sister Maria impatiently. "So, girls don't like flowers for Christmas," Winnie repeated incredulously. "But Well, they do like flowers, but not now!" Sister Maria answers a little more irritated. "Well, then not now," pouts Winnie. He carefully puts the flowers back in the bag. When he is finished, he looks at Sister Maria and says, "Now we can go." Sister Maria sighs again, and together with Winnie she makes her way to Lilly.

Arriving outside Lilly's room, Sister Maria knocks on the door. When nobody answers, she knocks again. But no one answers the second time. "Maybe she's decorating her room?" Winnie asks pleased. "Lilly and decorate? I am more like Santa Claus personally," replies Sister Maria and opens the door. "But there is already a Santa Claus," Winnie says in surprise. "Lilly! What are you doing?" asked Sister Maria angrily. But Lilly doesn't respond. Winnie looks past Sister Maria and sees a little girl with headphones in her ears, singing, lying on the bed. "She sings, too. That's nice!" Winnie claps his hands with joy. Sister Maria looks at him admonishingly and goes loudly to Lilly's bed. "Lilly! Turn off the music immediately!" Sister Maria now scolds louder. Unaffected, Lilly takes the headphones out of her ears. "What's going on now, penguin?" Lilly asks annoyed. "What is up? You lie in bed with shoes and listen to music. That's what's going on!" Sister Maria is furious. "My shoes, my bed! Clear?" Lilly answers indifferently. Only now does she notice that Sister Maria didn't come into the room alone.

She jumps up, "Who is that, and what does it do in my room?" Lilly calls out loud. "Lilly, this is Winnie. Winnie comes straight from Santa Claus, especially to you," Sister Maria replies with a smile and looks at Winnie. Winnie sees Lilly's cheeks flush. "What is he doing here and why the…why does he look like this?" Lilly storms. "You know, Lilly, Winnie is a Christmas Elf, and he should bring you closer to Christmas," Sister Maria still replies with a smile. "Santa Claus, Christmas Elf, and Christmas. Cheers to the three C's," says Lilly sarcastically. "I can see you are very pleased. Well then, I'll leave you alone now so that you can get to know each other," says Sister Maria cheerfully. "She only pretends to be angry," Sister Maria tries to explain to Winnie. "Well, see you later!" she says and leaves the room. Winnie and Lilly are left alone and stare at each other. "Listen, goblin, I…" "I'm not a goblin. I'm a Christmas Elf," Winnie interrupts Lilly. "When I say you're a goblin,

37

you're a goblin," says Lilly firmly, staring deeply into Winnie's eyes. Winnie thinks for a moment and replies, "All right, Lillifee." He laughs. Lilly snorts with anger, "Don't call me Lillifee!" "When I say you're Lillifee, you're Lillifee," says Winnie amused. Lilly struggles to compose herself. "You're bad and mean," she says, throwing herself angrily on her bed. In order not to hear Winnie, she puts the headphones back in her ears and starts singing loudly. Winnie looks around Lilly's room. "As desolate as my room. No wonder you get so nasty here," he says to himself. Winnie's gaze falls on a football book lying on the table by the window.

He goes purposefully and takes it in his hand. Lilly, who has been watching Winnie all the time, jumps up and rips the book from his hand. "This is my book! Don't touch it!" she scolds. Winnie looks at her incredulously. "Alright, Lillifee. You already know that this is a football book?"

"I know this is a football book. Why are you asking so stupid?" Lilly asks angrily. "And stop saying Lillifee to me," she warns Winnie. "Firstly, football is for boys, and you're a girl, and secondly, all girls like Lillifee," Winnie replies cheerfully. "But I'm not a girl, I can't stand Lillifee, and I love football. Winnie looks at Lilly incredulously. "You are a girl, or do you mean to say that you are a long-haired boy named Lilly? Lilli…fee." Lilly bangs her book angrily on the table. "Girls also can like football," she says defiantly. "By the way, you haven't apologized for always calling me Lillifee," she says without looking at Winnie. "You haven't apologized for calling me goblin yet," Winnie replies defiantly. "You can forget that, too.

I never apologize to anyone!" Lilly says firmly. So, she goes back to her bed and lies down on it. Again, she puts her headphones in her ears, but this time she doesn't sing along. Winnie sits down in the armchair and looks out the window. "Oh, I could just be at the sea," he thinks, sighing softly.

Half an hour later, Sister Maria comes back into the room. She looks around in surprise. "Everything is still complete here," she says with astonishment. "Why should something be broken?" Winnie asks, irritated. "Well, because Lilly doesn't usually last longer than five minutes without breaking something," Sister Maria replies. Lilly glares at Sister Maria. The latter ignores this and instead says, "I want to pick you two up for dinner."

"Oh great, finally without this goblin," Lilly replies cheerfully and leaves the room.

On the way to the dining room, Sister Maria looks at Winnie, "Santa Claus called earlier. He asks how you are and whether you want to go back home." Winnie thinks for a moment and then replies, "You can tell him that I am fine and that I will stay a little longer. My job is not yet done." Sister Maria nods.

Arrived in the dining room, Lilly looks at her seat. "What does that mean? Why are there two plates and glasses," she wants to know. "Because Winnie is sitting at the table with you," Sister Maria answers firmly. Lilly puts her hands on her waist. "But I don't want the goblin to sit with me!" she says angrily. "Again, I'm not a goblin, Lillyfee!" says Winnie defiantly. "Lillyfee!" repeated one of the children. All the children immediately start laughing and shout, "Lillyfee! Lillyfee!" Lilly's cheeks are red with anger. "You're mean," she yells at Winnie, "you're all mean!" She leaves the dining room in tears. "Now calm down!" Sister Maria warns the children. "There is no laughing at others!" she adds seriously. Secretly, however, she thinks something is going to happen to Lilly. Usually she annoys the children, makes fun of them, makes them cry, takes their things away, or breaks their things. None of the children ever dare to say anything to Lilly or to defend herself. When Winnie sees that Lilly started crying because of him, he feels guilty and runs after her.

On the way to her room, Lilly passes Winnie's room. Determined, she opens the door and goes purposefully to the window to tear off the colorful flowers. Just when she wants to destroy Winnie's beach picture, he comes running into the room.

"What are you doing there? My things!" he calls startled. "You are so mean! Stop it immediately!" He tries to stop Lilly. However, Lilly doesn't think about it and pulls Winnie's beach picture from the wall. In anger, she tears it up in front of his eyes. Now Winnie starts to cry. Determined he runs into Lilly's room, takes her soccer book, and breaks it, too. He scatters the individual pages in her room. When Lilly sees this, she starts screaming, "This is my book! You broke my book!" With tears, she pulls the rest of the book out of Winnie's hands. "Do you know how long I saved for that?" she cries and throws herself on her bed. She starts to sob loudly. "Do you know how long it took me for my picture?" Winnie asks sadly and leaves the room.

When he arrives in his room, he looks at the chaos. Sister Maria, who has heard everything, tries to comfort him, "I am very sorry, Winnie. I should have seen that coming." Winnie wipes the tears from his eyes. "That's fine. I'll do everything again," he says sadly. Sister Maria caresses his head. "I brought your food to your room. You can eat here if you want to." Winnie nods and thanks. When Sister Maria is out of the room, Winnie starts tidying up and redecorating everything. Then he sits down at the table and begins to eat. He thinks about Lilly's words that she had to save for the book for so long. Even if he still doesn't understand why a girl has a soccer book, and it actually happens that her book is broken now, he has a guilty conscience. "Just because Lilly is so mean, I don't have to be mean," he thinks. After a short hesitation, he gets up, goes to his easel, and begins to paint. He paints the most beautiful soccer he has ever seen. He then goes to Lilly's room and is about to knock on the door when he hears Lilly's crying from inside. Winnie's guilty conscience grows even bigger. He pushes the picture under the door and says softly, "Sorry, Lilly!"

Winnie obviously said this loudly enough that Lilly could hear it. From the inside she exclaims exhausted, "Go away! I do not want to see you! Never again!" Sadly, Winnie goes back to his room. There he gets ready for bed and goes to sleep. For the first time Winnie can remember, he doesn't   sing   himself   to   sleep.

Lilly now has seen Winnie's picture. Actually, she wanted to tear it up because she is so angry and sad at the same time. "Why is he painting me a picture? And why is he sorry?" she wonders. "I started it. Nobody has ever apologized to me when I started it," Lilly states irritatedly. For the first time, Lilly feels something that she cannot name. She actually feels sad about what she's done. She sits on her bed for a long time and thinks about what happened before finally she sleeps, too.

The next morning, after a restless night for both, Winnie and Lilly sit opposite each other in silence at the breakfast table. Nobody dares to look at the other. Sister Maria notices that Lilly eats calmly and properly for the first time in a long time. It's almost like she's not there.

After Lilly has finished eating and cleared away her dishes, she also goes to her room in silence. There she begins to pack her backpack. Winnie, who wants to try again to talk to Lilly, can just see her climbing out of her window. He quickly runs into his room, grabs his coat and backpack, and runs to the front door.

After skillfully breaking the door security, he runs outside. He looks frantically to the right and left and then sees Lilly's braids in the distance. He runs as fast as he can and actually manages to catch up with her after a short time.

Out of breath he arrives next to her. Lilly is startled, "Winnie, what are you doing here?" Still out of breath, Winnie answers, "I could ask you the same thing."

"I'm running away from this stupid orphanage." Winnie can't believe his ears, "But Lilly, you can't do that, it's too dangerous," replies Winnie, startled. "I don't care. I've run away so many times. Nothing ever happened to me," Lilly replies carefree. "But why are you actually here?" she asks Winnie with irritation. "Well, because I can't leave you alone," replies Winnie. "So, you think I can't do it on my own?" Lilly asks sarcastically. Winnie thinks. "Well, if you've run away many times and nothing ever happened, then you will probably be fine   on   your   own."

"Then you can go again," says Lilly. "But if I want to stay with you because I like you?" Winnie asks quietly. Lilly stops in shock and looks at Winnie. "Never say you like me, ok? You can say anything you want. You can scold me and say that I'm stupid, mean, and bad, but never say you like me."

"Are you going to break something of me when I say I like you?" Winnie asks carefully. Lilly hesitates, then says, "Listen, nobody likes me, ok? Nobody has ever liked me, and it will always be like that." Winnie wonders why Lilly thinks so but keeps the question to himself for now.

After walking a few feet further, Lilly looks at Winnie again, "I won't get rid of you, will I?" Winnie shakes his head, "No, you won't get rid of me for now," he confirms. "Great," says Lilly softly and continues towards the city center.

After a while she also says softly, "Thank you for not calling me Lillyfee anymore."

"Oh you know, in your eyes I may just be a stupid goblin, but I'm not angry," replied Winnie sadly. Lilly swallows. "Somehow I'm sorry I was so angry with Winnie," she thinks, "but I just can't apologize. Apologizing means showing weakness, and I am not weak."

After they have left for a while, Lilly wonders if it is really a weakness to apologize. Somehow she's afraid of it, but she can't talk to Winnie about it, at least not yet. "I'm hungry," says Winnie suddenly. "Me, too," replies Lilly. "But we don't have anything to eat, or did you take something with you?" Winnie asks. Lilly shakes her head, "No, unfortunately, I didn't, and if you must ask, then you probably don't have any food either, right?!" Winnie shakes his head. "Ok, watch out. I'll take care of it." And Lilly has disappeared into a bakery. After she comes out, she commands Winnie, "Go, Winnie, Run!" Without knowing what happened, Winnie runs and follows Lilly into a small alley. Completely out of breath, she holds out a

Gingerbread Man to him. "Here. It is for you," she gasps. "Thanks, but why are we running like that?" Winnie wants to know. Lilly looks back and forth uneasily, "It doesn't matter. Just eat", she directs Winnie. Just when Winnie wanted to bite the Gingerbread Man, he got a strange feeling. "Lilly! Did you steal it?" Winnie asks in shock.

"Well, do you have any money with you?" Lilly asks flatly. "No, but that's why you can't steal," replies Winnie. "Come on. We'll take them back," he tells Lilly. "Are you crazy? We're hungry," Lilly replies, irritated. "Yes, but there has to be another way," says Winnie firmly. When Lilly sees that Winnie is serious, she puts her Gingerbread Man back in the bag and starts walking. "How are we supposed to bring it back now? They'll snap us straight away and take us back to the orphanage," Lilly explains helplessly. "How about you apologize and explain to them that we are hungry?"

"Should I apologize?"

"Yes, I know this is not exactly your favorite task, but it has to be now."

"Why should I do that?" Lilly wants to know. "Because I don't believe you are as bad as you always say you are," Winnie replies firmly. "Ouch! That hurt!" thinks Lilly. Arriving in front of the bakery, Lilly hesitates for a moment. "Come on. I'm with you," says Winnie, holding out her hand.

When the door opens and a woman comes out, Lilly takes Winnie's hand anxiously and goes in with him. At the counter, she recognizes the woman she stole from earlier. Lilly looks anxiously at Winnie, who winks at her. Lilly looks down. "It…it…well…I wanted to say that, well…," Lilly hesitates. "I can't do that, Winnie!" Lilly says desperately. "Yes, you can," he encourages her. Suddenly Lilly starts to cry, "I'm sorry. I didn't want to be dishonest. We're just hungry, and we don't have any money." Lilly can no longer calm down. The saleswoman comes around the counter. "Oh, little one, don't cry. It's all good. You were so honest and brought the food back. I accept your apology." The shop assistant leans down to Lilly and strokes her head. With this gesture, Lilly is startled and immediately stiffens. The seller notices this and immediately releases

Lilly. "You know what, little one, I invite you and your little friend to dinner. Sit down at the table and eat your Gingerbread Man in peace. I'll bring you two more cups of chocolate with cream. You like hot chocolate, don't you?" asks the shop assistant with a smile. Winnie and Lilly nod gratefully and relived and sit down at the free table in the corner.

After the saleswoman is back and has placed the cups in front of Winnie and Lilly, Lilly looks to the floor in shame and fear. "Are you calling the police now?" she asks quietly. The shop assistant shakes her head, "No, little one, I am not calling the police." The shop assistant knows that Lilly is out of the orphanage and regularly runs away.

"Now drink your hot chocolate in peace and have your Gingerbread Man. I'll be right back to you." With these words, the saleswoman disappears into the room behind the sales counter. There she calls the orphanage and informs Sister Maria about the events. Sister Maria is very irritated about Lilly's actions and so, after consulting with Santa Claus, decides not to bring Lilly back to the orphanage.

Ten minutes later, the saleswoman comes back to Winnie and Lilly. "Well, did you like it?" she asks kindly. "Yes, very good, thank you!" Winnie also answers kindly. "And you, little one?" asked the saleswoman. Lilly just nods. She is too ashamed of what happened. "You look like you have a long journey ahead of you. I would like to give you a piece of cake and a juice of your choice on the way." Lilly cannot believe what the saleswoman has just said and so she looks at her for the first time. The saleswoman recognizes a deep sadness in Lilly's eyes. "What do you want for a piece of cake, little one?" asks the seller lovingly. Lilly cannot answer. The situation is so unusual for her. The saleswoman looks at Winnie. "Do you know what you want?" she asks him. "So, I love cheesecake," he says, beaming all over his face. "Well, a cheesecake for you and…," she looks at Lilly again. "One apple pie, please," Lilly says quietly. The shop assistant smiles. "So, a cheesecake and an apple pie. And the drinks?" she asks. Winnie and Lilly order an orange and an apple juice. When the saleswoman puts things together, Lilly looks at Winnie. "We have nothing to say thank you," she says with shame. Winnie thinks for a moment. "But, of course, we have something." He carefully pulls his bag of colorful flowers out of his backpack. When looking at the many colorful flowers, Lilly looks confused, "Why do you have all the flowers?"

"I love flowers," replies Winnie. "Yes, but you're a Christmas Elf. You have to like Christmas things," Lilly says. "Yes, and you're a girl, so you have to like girls' clothes and not soccer," Winnie replies defiantly. Lilly wonders if she and Winnie aren't as different as it looks at first glance. "Quick! Pick a flower!" Winnie asks Lilly. Lilly sees that the saleswoman is coming back and quickly decides on a purple flower. Winnie takes a red flower out of the bag. When the seller has put everything on the table, Lilly gets up and holds the flower out to her. "It is not Christmassy now, but we have nothing else. We would like to give you the flowers."

"Yes, exactly," says Winnie, who also gets up to give the seller the flower. Touched by this gesture, the shop assistant leans down and hugs Winnie to say thank you. Lilly, who watches the whole thing carefully, plays restlessly with her hands and tugs on her coat. The saleswoman turns to Lilly and holds out her hand. "I know you obviously don't like being touched," she says with a smile, thinking of the situation when she patted Lilly on the head.

To surprise the saleswoman, Lilly suddenly falls into her arms and presses firmly against her. Winnie is also surprised by Lilly's reaction and looks at them with wide eyes and an open mouth. The saleswoman lovingly puts her arms around Lilly and gently strokes her back. "You are a lovely girl," she says quietly. Lilly immediately frees herself from the hug, looks at the floor, and shakes her head. "No, I'm not a lovely girl. I'm angry," she replies, takes the cake and juice, and runs out. Winnie, who is still standing there with his mouth open, asks, "What was that about?" The saleswoman, who looked at Lilly pityingly, looks at Winnie, "You know, little fellow, the little one has obviously been very hurt. Because of this, she has built a wall around herself and cannot allow any feelings." The seller pauses for a moment, then continues, "The children who grow up in the orphanage usually have very difficult or unfortunate fates. The little one will probably feel offended and think she's in the orphanage because she's bad."

"But I don't think Lilly is angry. She only pretends to be angry," says Winnie with conviction. The saleswoman pats Winnie on the head. "And I'm sure you're right," she confirms. "But what can you do about it?" Winnie wants to know. The shop assistant sighs, "You can only do that by building trust with a lot of time and patience," she explains. Winnie thinks. "I want to try to help her," he says firmly. "You know what, little guy? I even think you can do it," says the saleswoman. Winnie's eyes widen again, "Why can I do this?" he wonders. The saleswoman laughs, "Do you know how often the little girl has robbed me? She never came back to bring anything back, least of all to apologize." Winnie looks at the door. "I didn't know that," he says quietly. The seller hands Winnie his piece of cake and the orange juice. "Go to her. She's definitely waiting for you," the saleswoman kindly tells Winnie. "Do you think?"

Winnie asks a little incredulously. "I'm sure of it," replies the seller. Winnie takes the piece of cake and the orange juice, carefully packs both in his backpack, and says thank you. When he went out, the shop assistant called after him, "I would be happy if I would see you both again." Winnie turns around, looks at the shop assistant, and says, "We'll be back, I promise!" Then he leaves the bakery and sets off to find Lilly.

Winnie runs to the little alley where Lilly gave him the Gingerbread Man earlier. "How did you find me?" Lilly asks angrily. "It wasn't that difficult now," replies Winnie. "Why did you run away?" "I didn't run away," Lilly still answers angrily. "But it looked very different, just now," says Winnie. "Oh, leave me alone, you don't understand that anyway." With these words, Lilly leaves Winnie and walks back towards the city center. "Fine, then I just don't understand it, but can I at least come with you anyway?" Winnie argues. "You're doing what you want anyway," Lilly calls back without turning around. Winnie immediately runs to go with Lilly.

As they walk, Lilly keeps looking carefully in all directions. "Why do you always look around like that?" Winnie wants to know. "Well, why do you, clever head?" asks Lilly. Winnie knows but shrugs. "Maybe because I left and they are looking for me again!" Lilly answers annoyed. "Sounds logical on the one hand, but not on the other," says Winnie. "What's that supposed to mean?" asks Lilly. "Well, if you're so bad and mean, they can actually be happy that you're gone," Winnie replies thoughtfully. Lilly wrinkles her nose, "You are so mean," she says and runs again. Winnie can barely see Lilly's eyes filling with tears again. He sighs and runs after her again.

Lilly stops short of a church and takes several deep breaths. "Can't I get rid of you?" she asks annoyed. Winnie thinks of what the saleswoman told him. "Yes, you will," he says then, "you just have to tell me to go away instead of always running away yourself. Because then I don't know that you want to get rid of me," he adds. Lilly's gaze falls on a couple of parents holding their little daughter by the hand and happily going to church with her.

Winnie sees Lilly sadly looking after them. After a few minutes, she asks, "So if I tell you to go, will you go and leave me alone forever?" Winnie thinks for a moment. "If Lilly sends me away, I could just go because it's her wish." He thinks again very firmly of what the saleswoman told him, "Maybe I shouldn't go because Lilly really doesn't want it? Maybe she just can't say that I should stay with her because she expects everyone to leave her…"

"Hello? Are you still there, or are you mentally sitting with Santa Claus again?" Lilly interrupts Winnie's thoughts. "You know, Lilly, I was just thinking about it, if you send me away and it's really your wish, I'll go," Winnie replies. "But?" Lilly asks somewhat uncertainly. Winnie looks Lilly in the eye, "No but. You just have to tell me."

"Fine, then I want you to go. I never want to see you again," says Lilly in a shaky voice. "As you wish, Lilly. Farewell!" With these words, Winnie turns and heads for the church. Lilly watches him with concern. She's starting to cry. "Why am I crying now? It's just a Christmas Elf who doesn't like me either…one of many," thinks Lilly. Lilly sees Winnie disappear into the church. "And if I really never see him again now?" she thinks. And as before in the bakery, she begins to knead her hands and pluck her coat. "Oh, then that's the way it should be," she says angrily and leaves.

After walking for a while, she passes a soccer field. With determination, she walks through the gate and sits on one of the benches. A couple of boys are playing soccer on the soccer field. Lilly watches them with interest. "Why do I have to think of Winnie all the time?" she wonders sadly. "He just left and left me alone," Lilly says angrily to herself. "You said that I should go, and you never want to see me again," a voice sounds behind her. Startled, Lilly turns. "Winnie!" she says happily and jumps up. "Oh, what's that?" Winnie asks in surprise. "You're happy to see me?" Lilly looks back and forth uncertainly. "Yes, no…well…maybe," she replies quietly. "Oh you know, Lilly, I'm happy to see you, too," sighs Winnie and sits next to Lilly on the bench. Lilly also sits down again. "Why are you so happy? I mean, I sent you away." Winnie nods. "Yes, you did…"

"But?" Lilly interrupts him. "Even if you don't want to hear it, Lilly, I really like you," replies Winnie. Lilly looks down. "Why do you say something like that? Nobody likes me. Not even my parents like me." "Why do you say that, Lilly?" Winnie asks. "Why else have I been in the orphanage for eight years? I came to the orphanage when I was four months old and have never seen my parents. All other children see their parents. Only I don't see mine. So, I must have been very awful that my parents no longer like me and don't even want to see me anymore," says Lilly sadly and starts crying. "Have you ever asked about your parents?" Winnie offers sympathetically. Lilly shakes her head, "No, I haven't," she replies. "But why not?" Winnie wants to know. "If my parents don't care about me, then I don't care about them either!" Lilly replies unconvincingly. Winnie sighs, "I have to find out what about Lilly's parents," he thinks. Both watch the boys playing soccer. "Why do you like soccer so much?" asks Winnie. "I just think it's nice. It's a lot of fun," Lilly replies with a glow in her eyes. "So, then you've played soccer a lot?" Winnie inquires. Lilly shakes her head and looks down. "No, frankly, never," she replies sadly. "Whaaat? You love soccer, but have never played soccer yourself?" Winnie asks in surprise. "Well, where am I supposed to play soccer?" Lilly replies hopelessly. "Oh, wait! We'll fix it right away." With one sentence, Winnie jumps off the bench and heads for the field. Startled, Lilly hurries after him. "Winnie, what are you up to?" she calls after him. Without answering, Winnie enters the field. "Hello, boys, can someone play with you?" he asks. The boys stop abruptly. They look at Winnie and start laughing. "So, what do you look like?" "You want to play soccer?" Winnie shakes his head, "No, not me. My friend Lilly wants to play with you." The boys laugh even louder. "A girl want to play soccer," says the tallest of the boys. "Do you even know what soccer is?" asks another. "And the little goblin has to ask for the girl," says the third. Lilly sees that Winnie is feeling sad and close to tears. She quickly stands next to him. "Leave Winnie alone. Winnie is my friend!" she says angrily. "Sure, your friend," laughs the tall one. Lilly stands in front of the big boy. "Watch out, you stupid man. Winnie is my friend, and he's not a goblin. He's a Christmas Elf," Lilly says in a sharp tone. "Ok, ok, little girl, calm down!" the big boy replies with a laugh.

Not taking his eyes off the big boy, Lilly suddenly kicks the ball under his foot and starts running. "Hey, are you crazy?" the big boy calls after her. "What? Are you a little afraid of a girl, you stupid man?" Lilly calls back. The boys run after Lilly and try to take the ball from her. Lilly skillfully plays the ball around her and shoots it towards Winnie. "Here, Winnie, take!" she calls. Winnie takes the ball and looks at Lilly. "Run towards the gate, Winnie!" she coaches him and points to the gate to his right. Winnie runs and shoots the ball in front of him. Just as the big boy takes the ball from Winnie, Lilly runs in between and kicks the ball back. She turns around on her own axis and plays the ball around two other boys who are just running.

She runs purposefully towards the gate. The big boy has caught up with Lilly and wants to take the ball from her again when Lilly sinks the ball into the goal by another turn. The boys remain confused and cannot believe their eyes. "Has she really scored a goal now?" one of the boys asks incredulously. "Yes, I'm afraid," answers another. "She really prevailed against the five of us now?" one asks. "Yes, she did," the other nods. "Your goalkeeper is not exactly the best," cries Lilly, turning around. "Come on, Winnie, we're going!" she asks him. Winnie, who is also completely impressed by Lilly's performance, walks next to her. "And you are sure that you have never played soccer before?" he asks with a laugh. Lilly laughs back, "No, not really," she replies. The big boy catches up with them just before they reach the gate. "Hey, wait a minute!" he calls. Lilly turns around. "What is? You have your ball again!" she answers with a sharp tone. The big boy looks uncertainly between Lilly and Winnie. "Our goalkeeper is really not the best," he says. "Yes, and?" Lilly wants to know. "We still have a pair of goalkeeper gloves," says the tall boy shyly. "And you think your friend can play better with it?" laughs Lilly. "Maybe you want to play along?" says the big boy softly. "I want something?" Lilly asks irritated. "He's asking if you want to play," says Winnie happily, clapping his hands. "Yes, I understood that already," says Lilly, "but why do you ask that?" she wants to know from the big boy. The big boy is getting nervous. "Are you playing now or not?" he still asks uncertainly. "But it has to be a big deal for you to ask a girl," Lilly tries to annoy the big boy. "Then don't," replies the big boy and turns around. "Hey, I didn't say no," Lilly replies. "Cool…I mean…good," says the big boy shortly. He looks at Winnie. "Are you playing, too?" he asks him kindly. "Oh no, I'd rather watch you," Winnie replies cheerfully and runs back to the benches. Lilly and the big boy head for the field.

"My name is Jonas, by the way," says the big boy. "I'm Lilly," she replies with a smile. After the other guys introduced themselves to Lilly, it starts. Jonas gives her a pair of goalkeeper gloves, which Lilly takes with a beam of joy. "Have you ever stood in the gate?" Jonas asks. Lilly shakes her head, "No, never," she replies. "Well, if you are as natural talent at goalkeeping as you are at scoring a goal, then we will have a hard time," he says, winking at Lilly. They start playing less than two minutes later. Winnie watches everything closely and is happy about every ball because Lilly catches them all. "Super, Lilly! Great! Yes, keep it up," he exclaims again and again enthusiastically from the bank and cheerfully claps his hands.

After an hour, everyone is completely out of breath. "Wow! You're good!" says one of the guys, who has introduced himself as Johannes. "Yes, you are," Jonas agrees. Happy and satisfied, Lilly returns the goalkeeper gloves to Jonas. "Thank you, guys. It was really fun playing with you," Lilly says and heads for Winnie. Winnie runs towards her beaming with joy. "Lilly, you did it so well," he says, clapping his little hands again.

Just when Winnie and Lilly to the gate, Jonas calls them back, "Hey, you two, wait a minute!" Winnie and Lilly turn around. "Will you come over again?" he asks Lilly. "We really can use a cool goalkeeper woman like you," added Jonas shyly. "I thought girls couldn't play soccer," Lilly replies sarcastically. "Now don't sprinkle salt in the wound," says Jonas, looking down at the floor. After a moment's hesitation, he looks back at Lilly. "So? Will you come over again?" he tries again. Lilly looks at Winnie, who nods with joy. "I don't think that works," Lilly replies sadly and turns to the exit. "Think about it!" Jonas calls after her. Without answering, Lilly leaves the soccer field. Winnie, who was still looking back and forth between Lilly and Jonas, shrugs his shoulders apologetically and runs to Lilly.

"Why did you say you wouldn't come back? It was so much fun for you," Winnie demands. "Imagine if they know that I come from the orphanage. They will definitely find it completely repulsive," replies Lilly. "Why should they?" Winnie still asks firmer. "Because orphans are problems and outcasts," Lilly replies sadly, "Nobody likes orphans."

"That's not true. I like you!" Winnie answers resolutely. Lilly sighs and then continues in silence.

After a while, Winnie asks, "Are you hungry?" Lilly nods. "Yes, very! What should we eat?" Winnie thinks for a moment. "We still have the cake from the bakery," replies Winnie with shining eyes. "That's right, Winnie," Lilly is also pleased.

"Come on, we're looking for a place to eat the cake," suggests Lilly. Winnie nods. "Good."

Just when they have found a place and want to sit down, their gaze falls on a homeless person. Winnie looks at Lilly. "Lilly, do you think the man is hungry, too?" he asks sympathetically. Lilly looks at the man. "Yes, I think so," she replies. "Should we share our food with him?" suggests Winnie. Lilly nods, "Yes, that is a good idea. We have enough for the three of us." Winnie and Lilly walk over to the man. "What now?" Lilly asks quietly. "Talk to him," Winnie also replies quietly. "I do not trust myself. Do it, Winnie," Lilly prompts Winnie. Winnie thinks for a moment and speaks to the man. "Hello!" he greets him. "I'm Winnie, and this is my friend Lilly," he introduces The man looks at the two with annoyance. "I have nothing I can give you," he then says. Winnie shakes her head, "Oh, no, we don't want anything. We want to give you something," Winnie tries to explain. The man still looks confused. Winnie puts

74

his little backpack on the floor and pulls out the piece of cheesecake. "You look hungry, and that's why we want to give you a piece of cake," says Winnie, smiling at the man. The man looks at the bag. "Don't you like cake?" Winnie asks uncertainly. "If you don't like cheesecake, Lilly has an apple pie. Maybe you want it instead?" Winnie tries again. The man shakes his head, "No, it is not. I just don't remember the last time I ate a piece of cake," the man says quietly. Winnie and Lilly look shocked. "But you can always eat cake," says Lilly finally. The man shakes his head again, "If you live on the street, you can rarely eat a piece of cake. And then only when someone has thrown it away and you can find it," explains the man sadly. "Now you get a piece of cake," says Winnie and sits next to the man. "So, cheesecake or apple pie?" he asks cheerfully. "It's a difficult decision," the man replies uncertainly. "Then you just get a piece from both of us," says Lilly and also sits next to the man. "It's a good idea," agrees Winnie. Winnie and Lilly break off a piece of their cake and hand it to the man. "Bon Appetit," wishes Lilly. After Winnie and the man had also wished them a good appetite, they all relished biting into their cake. "Ah, I just remembered something," says Winnie, pulling the bottle of orange juice out of his little backpack. "We still have some juice." "Oh, yes, that's right," Lilly confirms and also pulls her juice bottle out of the backpack. Both successively pour some of their juice into the plastic cup that sits in front of the man. He thanks him and then slowly drinks the mug.

After eating and drinking, Winnie looks at the man and asks, "Why are you actually homeless?" The man sighs, "You know, I actually had everything. A beautiful and lovely woman, two very good and great girls, a nice house, and a great job…" "That sounds very good," interrupted Winnie. "Yes, that's right," agrees Lilly. "Yes, that was very nice," confirms the man. "Then what happened?" Lilly prods. "You know, I didn't realize I was going to lose my family."

"How can you lose your family?" Winnie asks in astonishment. "When you work and work even more and work even more. Everything to make it nice for your family," the man hesitates briefly, "and of course for yourself," he adds. "In any case, I didn't notice how I had less and less time for my family. My wife was very much alone with the children and at some point she gave me the choice."

"Which choice?" asks Lilly. "Yes, which choice?" Winnie also wants to know. "The choice was either I cut back on work or I lose my family," the man replies. "You chose your family, didn't you?" Winnie asks excitedly. The man lowers his head, "I thought my wife was not serious, and everything calmed down again…I thought she gets used to it," he replied quietly. Lilly looks at the empty plastic cup and then at the paper cup that contains a few coins. "It hasn't calmed down again, has it?" Winnie asks. The man shakes his head. "No, not everything has calmed down again," he confirms. "Then what happened?" Lilly continues. "My wife packed her and the girls' things and wanted to move out. I tried to talk to her, tried to stop her, but hopelessly. She didn't want to stay with me anymore. I begged her to at least stay in the house with the girls." "Has she stayed?" Winnie asked quietly. "Yes, she stayed," the man confirms, "but I left," he replies. "But that's sad," says Winnie. "Yes, very sad," agrees Lilly. "Then what happened?" Winnie asks. "In the beginning, I lived in a small apartment, and

I worked even more than before. But I quickly realized that my yearning for my wife and daughters was growing. I tried talking to my wife a few more times and tried to change her mind…" "But she didn't go for it!" Lilly interrupts him quietly. "That's right. She didn't respond," the man confirms and starts to cry. Winnie and Lilly look at each other sadly. "But why are you living on the street now?" Winnie asks. "At some point, I just couldn't go any further. I lost my job and the apartment, so I sat on the street," explains the man. "But didn't you try to talk to your wife anymore?" Lilly wonders. The man shakes his head, "No, since I have been living on the street and that has been three years now, I have not spoken to her," he says sadly. "Why not? Maybe you still have a chance," Lilly tries to comfort the man. "She didn't talk to me before, so she won't talk to me now," explains the man. "Besides, what does a woman want from a man who lives on the street?" he asks quietly. "I think you should try

79

again," says Lilly firmly. "Yes, I think so, too," agrees Winnie. "And if it doesn't work again?" the man asks hopelessly. "Then at least you did everything you could do. And honestly," Lilly looks again at the paper cup with the coins, "What could be worse?" The man thinks, "I could lose my dignity?" Lilly looks at him skeptically. "Seriously now?" Now the man also looks at the paper cup and at the few things that are left to him. "How can such a little girl and such a little Christmas Elf find such wise words?" he asks in defeat. "We're just a good team," laughs Lilly. "That's right," says Winnie happily. Lilly's gaze falls on a little boy who received a coin from his mother to put in the man's mug. The man thanks him and smiles sadly at the little boy. "Not much comes together, does it?" Lilly asks sadly. "It is enough to have one hot meal a day," replies the man.

"I have an idea," says Winnie cheerfully, "we can sing something. You can do it so well, Lilly." "I do not know. I don't think what I can sing is right for Christmas." She looks uncertainly at Winnie. "Can you sing something?" she asks him. "So," Winnie thinks, "I can sing "All the Birds are Already There," "Under the Sea," "Hiking is the Miller's Delight", the "Lava" Song…" "Um, Winnie, you already know that it's Christmas, don't you?" Lilly asks skeptically. Winnie thinks. "Do you know a Christmas carol?" he asks the man. "My wife and my children liked

"Silent Night, Holy Night,'"" he replies sadly. "I know that," says Lilly happily. "Me, too," says Winnie cheerfully. "Then we'll sing together," suggests Lilly. "I don't know," says the man uncertainly, "do you really mean it?" "Well, of course!", answered Winnie and Lilly together. The man sighs, "All right, together."

"Silent night, holy night! All is calm, all is bright – Round yon Virgin, Mother and Child – Holy Infant so tender and mild – Sleep in heavenly peace – Sleep in heavenly peace."

The three see that more and more people are joining them. Some of them start to sing along.

"Silent night! Holy night! Son of God, O how he laughs – Love from your divine mouth, Then it hits us – the hour of salvation. Jesus at your birth! Jesus at your birth!"

People come from all sides and join them. Many of them throw coins into the paper cup that is slowly filling up.

"Silent night! Holy night! Which brought salvation to the world, From Heaven's golden heights, Mercy's abundance was made visible to us: Jesus in human form, Jesus in human form."

In the crowd, Lilly suddenly sees a woman starting to cry. She holds two little girls in her arms.

"Silent night! Holy night! Where on this day all power of fatherly love poured forth – And like a brother lovingly embraced – Jesus the peoples of the world, Jesus the peoples of the world."

Lilly looks at the man and signals him to look into the crowd. The man follows Lilly's gaze and suddenly freezes.

"Silent night! Holy night! Already long ago planned for us, When the Lord frees from wrath – Since the beginning of ancient times – A salvation promised for the whole world. A salvation promised for the whole world."

Lilly sees the tears running down the woman's cheeks. The man also begins to cry. Lilly gets up, walks into the crowd, and shakes hands with the woman. Lilly takes her hand. Together with the woman's two daughters, they go to the man who has risen in the meantime.

"Silent night! Holy night! To shepherds it was first made known – By the angel, Alleluia; Sounding forth loudly far and near: Jesus the Savior is here! Jesus the Savior is here!" they all sing together.

"Henriette!"
"Friedrich!"

Winnie and Lilly look at each other with wide eyes. "What are we going to do now, Winnie?" Lilly asks quietly. "I don't know," Winnie replies just as quietly. "I think we're better off," Lilly suggests, and Winnie nods in agreement. Just when the two have taken their backpacks and want to go, the man stops them. "Hey, you two, wait a minute!" Winnie and Lilly turn to the man. He kneels to the ground. "Thank you for everything," he says, handing them the paper cup with the coins. "No, no, the money is for you," Lilly declines. "Exactly! We don't want that," agrees Winnie. The man looks into the paper cup. "Then take at least one coin or two," the man asks, holding out the paper cup to them. Winnie and Lilly look at each other. "Well, one," Lilly sighs and takes 25 cents from the mug. After Lilly takes the coin out of the cup, the man holds the cup up to Winnie and asks, "You too, little guy!" Winnie nods and takes 25 cents as well. Both thank him kindly. The man looks at her sadly. "You are so nice. How can I ever thank you?" Lilly puts her right hand on the man's shoulder, "Patch things up with your family. Family is more important than work," she says, looking at the man's wife and children. The man nods. "I will try to do everything in my power," he says solemnly and takes Lilly in his arms. Winnie sees that Lilly doesn't freeze for the first time when someone hugs her and smiles. Then the man turns to Winnie. "Come here, little guy, let yourself be squeezed!" He says and holds out his arms to Winnie. Winnie runs into the man's arms and hugs him tightly, too. "Take care, you two!" "You, too," reply Winnie and Lilly, and they set off to continue on their way. "Maybe we'll see each other again!" the man calls after them. "Yeah, maybe," agreed Winnie and Lilly.

After walking awhile, Winnie looks at Lilly. "Lilly, do you think the man can do it again?" he asks. "I don't know. I hope so," Lilly replies thoughtfully. They pass the church again, in front of which they have stood before. Lilly watches the people going to church. Sometimes there are individual people, sometimes a couple, and then again parents or grandparents; with their children or grandchildren disappearing through the heavy brown door. Winnie, who is watching Lilly, asks, "Would you like to go in, too?" Lilly's eyes widen in alarm. "Me?" she asks in disbelief. "No, I'm not going to a church." Lilly is about to go on when she is almost run over by a little girl. For a brief moment, Lilly looks angry. She doesn't like it when someone gets in her way or even runs around her. "Are you looking forward to Christmas, too?" asks the little girl cheerfully. "Me? No, I'm not looking forward to Christmas," Lilly answers firmly. Now the little girl looks at Lilly with big eyes. "How can you not look forward to Christmas?" she asks incredulously. Now the little girl's parents are standing next to her. Lilly looks nervously at Winnie. "I don't think Santa loves me very much," Lilly replies quietly. The little girl shakes her head, "No, I don't think so. Santa Claus loves everyone." She thinks for a moment. "You just have to be nice yourself, right, mom?" The mother nods and strokes her daughter's head. "That's right, little one," she replies lovingly. After a brief moment of silence, Lilly looks at the little girl's parents and clears her throat, "Well, yes, we have to go now," she says uncertainly. "Where are you going?" the little girl wants to know. "You know, my friend Winnie was about to go to church with me…We're going there now." "Oh, great, the church is beautiful. We were already there today," says the little girl happily. "Yes, churches are beautiful," Lilly replies, trying to smile. "Well then, Lilly, let's go!" says Winnie. "All right!" Lilly agrees and quickly says goodbye to the little girl and her parents. Together with Winnie she goes to the church.

Arriving in front of the heavy brown door, she wants to turn around and go again. "I wouldn't do that," laughs Winnie. "Why not?" Lilly asks irritated. "Look who's waving there," Winnie still laughs. Only now Lilly sees the little girl. "Oh, aren't you safe from her?" she asks annoyed. "Happy Christmas, little girl!" Lilly calls and also waves. Then she turns and purposefully goes to church.

Once inside, she stands still uncertain. Winnie, who has happily walked a few steps further, turns around, and when he sees Lilly no longer standing next to him, he runs back. "Um, why are you stopping, Lilly?" he wants to know. "I don't like churches," she whispers softly. Winnie looks confused. "Why not? They're so beautiful!" Lilly doesn't answer. Winnie thinks. "What do you think about lighting a candle for the homeless man?" he asks cheerfully. "How so? He's not dead," Lilly replies in surprise. "You don't just light candles when someone's dead, Lilly," Winnie tries to explain. "Yes, and what does that bring then?" Lilly asks. "Well, there are many reasons why you can light a candle. For example, when you think of someone, when you wish someone something good, when you are sick, or when you have a difficult test that you ask for help for," explains Winnie. Lilly looks at Winnie questioningly, "Fine, but now I still don't know what that should do," says Lilly sarcastically. "It's just something beautiful, and you feel good about it," Winnie tries to explain further. Lilly looks at the people who have just lit a candle. "But the candles cost money. Look, people are all putting money in the basket! We don't have anything," sighs Lilly. Winnie smiles and puts his little hand in his coat. "Look what we have left!" he says happily and shows Lilly the coin. "Oh, yes, that's right," Lilly is now also happy and takes her 25 cents coin out of her coat. "Come on!" Winnie asks Lilly and walks toward the candles. Lilly sighs again and then hesitantly follows Winnie when she sees that he is serious.

Arrived in front of the candles, both put their 25 cents coin in the basket and take one of the candles. "And now?" Lilly asks. "I don't have a lighter," she says quietly. "Neither do I," replies Winnie. A nun, who is sitting in the front row, notices how the two are at a loss at the candles. She gets up and walks over to them. "Ever lit a match?" she asks lovingly, holding out a matchbox to Winnie and Lilly. Winnie and Lilly startle because they haven't noticed that someone has joined them. When Lilly sees that it is a nun, she is startled again. "So terrible, my child!" says the nun gently. Lilly is desperately wondering if she has seen this nun at the orphanage before, but she can't remember her face. "Yes, my parents always said I was so frightened as a small child," Lilly lies and looks to reinforce her statement toward the exit, as if she were looking at her parents. The nun also looks towards the exit. "Your parents are out there?" the nun says when she sees that nobody is at the exit. Winnie, who has watched the whole situation, tries to help Lilly. "Well, I've never lit a match," he says thoughtfully. "Only the big elves can do that," he adds sadly. "Well, if that's the case, then I want to show you, little guy," says the nun affectionately and takes a match from the box. "Look, that's how it works!" says the nun, lighting the match. After blowing out the fire, she hands the box to Winnie. "Please try it!" she asks Winnie.

Winnie carefully takes out a match and tries to light it, and he succeeds after the second time. "Oh, it works," he says happily, bringing the burning match to the candle wick to light it. After blowing out the match, he looks at the nun. "Now it's Lilly's turn, right?" he says cheerfully. "But of course," the nun also replies cheerfully and turns to Lilly. "Here, my child!" she says and hands Lilly the box. Lilly sees that the nun doesn't take her eyes off her. "Does she suspect anything?" she wonders uncertainly. Lilly tries calmly to take the box. "Thank you very much!" she says quietly. After Lilly has also lit her candle, the nun looks at her. "Would you like to sit down with me a little longer?" she asks. "I think my parents are already waiting for us," Lilly lies again. The nun nods. "Naturally! Then I don't want to stop you", she says and looks Lilly in the eyes. Lilly turns her eyes to Winnie for help. He shrugs. Lilly looks towards the exit, then back to the candles. "OK! I have no parents! My parents gave me up because they didn't want me. I am an orphan. Just an evil orphan that nobody wants! And I ran away from the orphanage and never want to go back there. Satisfied?!" Lilly gushes. Without waiting for an answer, she looks at Winnie and says, "Come on, Winnie, we're leaving!" Winnie looks back and forth between Lilly and the nun. Just when he wants to start running because Lilly has already arrived in the middle of the aisle, she stops. "What has she got?" Winnie asks irritated, "Otherwise she never stops," he adds. The nun smiles at him. Without saying anything, Lilly comes back and sits on the bench in the front row. She looks sadly at the candles and then at the floor. Winnie runs to her and sits next to her. "Are you sad, Lilly?" he asks uncertainly. "I don't know. I think so," Lilly replies quietly. Now the nun sits down next to Lilly. "Would you like to talk about it, my child?" she asks caringly. Lilly holds her hands in front of her face and starts crying. Minutes of silence pass. Suddenly she starts talking. "I don't really want to be angry, and I don't do it on purpose. There is only…" she hesitates briefly, but then continues, "there is such an anger in my stomach. It has to get out somehow."

"Why are you angry, my child?" the nun asks caringly. "Because nobody likes me. My parents just gave me up when I was a little baby. I was only four months old. What can you do so badly at four months that you are sent to an orphanage? I couldn't even speak to say something bad, and I couldn't crawl or run to break something. I didn't hit anyone either. So why did I have to go to the orphanage?" Lilly asks in tears. Winnie, who listened in silence, also begins to cry softly. "Have you ever asked the orphanage why you are there?" asks the nun thoughtfully. "No," Lilly replies shortly. "Why didn't you do that?" Lilly wipes the tears from her eyes. "Because I don't want to hear that I'm in the orphanage because I was troublesome to my parents, and they didn't want me because of that," Lilly replies sadly. The nun
96

thinks. "You know, my child, I think you should ask." Lilly shakes her head, "No, I really don't want to hear it," she says firmly. "But what if there is a completely different reason why you are in the orphanage?" the nun continues trying. "What should there be for a reason? My parents don't like me and never want to see me again. That's why they never pick me up for Christmas to celebrate with them at home, as the other children are allowed to do with their parents." Winnie, listening attentively, suddenly understood what was wrong with Lilly. "Wait a minute, Lilly, you just don't like Christmas because you are reminded of your parents who don't take you out of the orphanage at Christmas and the other children are allowed to go home to their parents at Christmas?" he asks in astonishment. Lilly nods and cries again. "Yes, it happens often that the other children are allowed to go home to their remaining families, and I have to stay alone in the orphanage. I don't always want to be at the orphanage for Christmas. I also want to go home to people who love me," Lilly explains sadly. "But there is no one who loves me. Nobody brings me home for Christmas. I'm always alone." Winnie swallows. That that's why Lilly doesn't like Christmas. He never would have thought. "I have to help Lilly somehow," he thinks. "So, I think the penguin…" Winnie looks at the nun, "Oh, sorry," he says quietly. "Well, I think the nun is right. You should ask why you are in the orphanage," he agrees. "And what's that supposed to bring?" Lilly asks defiantly. "It will bring you the truth, my child!" explains the nun gently. For the first time, Lilly looks the nun straight in the eyes. "What does that mean?" she wants to know. "Go back, my child, and try to find the answer," the nun replies, rising from the bench. Before she leaves, she puts her right hand on Lilly's shoulder. "I wish you all the best and all the strength of the world, my child! You will make the right decision. I am sure of it!" The nun also places her right hand on Winnie's shoulder. "All the best to you, too, little guy. You have a big task, and you master it wonderfully!" says the nun and moves away from the two. Winnie and Lilly look after the nun.

After the nun has disappeared through the heavy brown door, Winnie looks incredulously at Lilly. "Has everything really happened now, and has she really gone?" he asks. "Yes, that's probably the case," Lilly replies thoughtfully. Both look silently at the candles.

After sitting quietly on the bench for a few minutes, Winnie looks at Lilly again. "What are we going to do now, Lilly?" Winnie wants to know. Lilly ponders. "I...well...maybe...I think we should go back to the orphanage," she replies quietly, looking down at the floor. Winnie looks at her questioningly. "Are you sure?" Lilly nods. "Yes, I think so." Winnie also nods. "Then let's go!" he asks Lilly and rises from the bench. Lilly also gets up, and together they go toward the exit. Before they go outside, Lilly turns around again. "You are right, Winnie, churches are beautiful," she says quietly. Winnie smiles.

After they left the church, it was getting dark. Winnie and Lilly walk silently side by side for a while. "You, Winnie, why aren't you like the other Christmas elves? And what about the flowers and the beach pictures?" Lilly asks carefully. "Oh, that's actually very easy," replies Winnie, "I just love spring so much. I think it's nice when the first flowers come, and everything shines so beautifully. I like it when it's colorful. You surely know that, don't you?" Winnie asks dreamily. Lilly nods. "Yes, of course," she agrees, "that's nice, too. But why the beach?" she wants to know. "Oh, you know, there is also Christmas where there are beaches. And at some point I saw a book about the most beautiful beaches, and there was really such a beautiful beach. I fell so in love with it!" enthuses Winnie. "In love with a beach? Really now?" Lilly asks incredulously. "Really! You cannot imagine what it looked like in the book. And, well, I've been repainting the beach ever since," explains Winnie. "Hmm," Lilly muses, "have you ever been there before, and where is the beach anyway?" Lilly asks. "Maldives!" Winnie replies dreamily, looking really in love. "Paint…what?" Lilly presses. "Maldives,"

101

repeated Winnie. "Haven't you heard that before?" he questions. Lilly shakes her head. "No, frankly, not," she replies apologetically. "That's not bad. Maybe one day I can show you the book!" Winnie offers. "That would be nice," agrees Lilly. "Have you ever been there?" Lilly repeats her question. Winnie shakes his head. "Unfortunately not. Only other Christmas elves are allowed to go there," he replies sadly. "Why is that?" Lilly wants to know. Winnie shrugs and lifts his little hands up a little. "I don't know. I don't think Santa Claus believes in me because I'm too young." Lilly starts laughing at that moment. "Sorry, Winnie, but if Santa really doesn't send you to your beach because of that, then he's not particularly smart!" she says firmly. Winnie's eyes widen in irritation. "Why not?" he wants to know. "Hello? Santa Claus sends you here all by yourself so that you are with me, but not to your beach because you may be too small for it? Honestly, I could have been much worse than any danger on the beach," Lilly tries to explain. Winnie thinks. "I have never seen it like this," he replies. "You know, you should ask him why you weren't allowed to go to your beach," Lilly suggests. "I don't know. What if Santa gets angry about this question?" Winnie asks uncertainly. "Yes, and what if I ask why I'm in the orphanage and Sister Maria tells me that I was a bad baby and my parents didn't want me?" Lilly replies defiantly. "Fine. You've won," sighs Winnie. "I will ask why."

"Go on," Lilly says happily. "So, what about you?" Winnie asks, grinning at Lilly. "I don't know what you mean," Lilly says stupidly. "Alright!" laughs Winnie, without taking his eyes off Lilly. "It's good. I'm thinking about it, alright?!" says Lilly, in mock irritation. "Go on," Winnie now repeats Lilly's words. Both look at each other and have to laugh.

After 15 minutes, they are standing in front of the large brick building. Lilly looks uncertainly at Winnie. "Do you think Sister Maria is very angry now?" she asks him a little fearfully. Winnie thinks. "You can't get away...On the other hand, we didn't break anything, we weren't angry, and we came back on our own. It can't be that bad, can it?" he answers uncertainly. "I stole the wake-up men," reminds Lilly Winnie. "Yes, that's right, but we also brought it back again." Lilli sighs. "You ring the bell, Winnie, I don't trust myself," she asks him. Winnie looks at Lilly, extends his left arm, and reaches for the rope with his little hand. "I'm doing it now!" he says firmly. Lilly nods. Winnie moves the rope back and forth, ringing the bell.

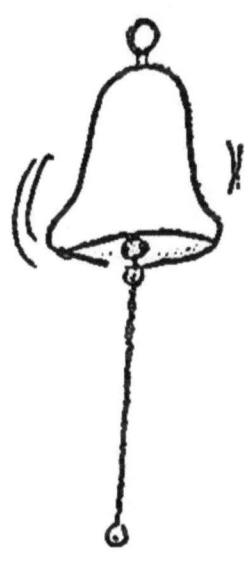

After the second ring, the door opens, and Sister
Maria stands in front of them. "I'm sorry. I'm
really sorry. I'm going to my room," Lilly
apologizes and runs past Sister Maria. Winnie stays
behind. He looks uncertainly at Sister Maria.
"Hello, Winnie, nice to have you back," Sister
Maria says kindly and looks at Winnie with a smile.
"But…but…aren't you angry at all?" Winnie asks
in astonishment. Sister Maria laughs and puts her
right hand on his shoulder. "No, I'm not. On the
contrary, I'm very happy that you both came back

on your own," she replies. "But I don't understand that now," says Winnie, confused. "Come on. I'll explain it to you!" Sister Maria explains. Together they go to Winnie's room.

"Go in and warm up a bit. It's very cold out there. I'll be right back," says Sister Maria caringly and continues down the hall. "Now that's odd," Winnie says quietly to himself and goes to his room. There he washes his hands and face, takes off his clothes, and puts on something warm and cozy. Then he sits down in the armchair by the window with a woolen blanket and a pillow. Shortly thereafter there is a knock on the door, and Sister Maria comes in. She has a tray in her hand. On it are a few slices of bread, some sausage and cheese, margarine, jam, and chocolate cream. Sister Maria also brought a large glass of milk and two mandarins. "You're definitely hungry after the long day!", she says and smiles at Winnie in a friendly way. "Can I have something to eat now?"

Winnie asks surprised. "Yes, but why not?" Sister Maria also asked in surprise. "Well, because we ran away from here and didn't say anything. Usually you have to go to bed without eating if you've done something wrong," explains Winnie. Sister Maria laughs, "But there is no prison here, and we are not in the Middle Ages either. Everyone has to eat and drink, no matter what they have done." Thankfully, Winnie takes the tray. "Will Lilly get something to eat and drink?" he asks carefully. "Of course," Sister Maria answers and strokes Winnie again, "I'm going to bring her something, too. Enjoy it, and we'll see you again later," she says and leaves the room. Winnie sighs with relief and begins to eat.

Sister Maria now goes to Lilly's room with a tray. She knocks on the door four times. When Lilly doesn't answer, Sister Maria enters the room. Unlike usual, Lilly is not lying on the bed with her shoes and headphones. Instead, she crawled deep into her blanket and turned her back to the door. When Sister Maria comes closer, she hears Lilly crying. She carefully places the tray on the table by the window and goes to Lilly.

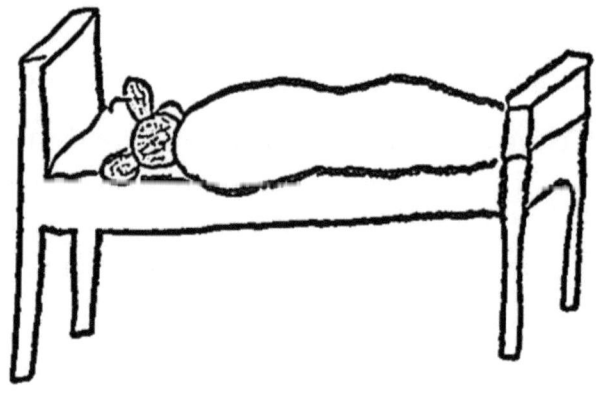

"Lilly, my child, why are you crying?" Sister Maria asks lovingly. Lilly doesn't answer and instead starts crying louder. Sister Maria sits next to her and strokes her head. "What's going on, my child?" Sister Maria tries again. Suddenly Lilly can no longer hold back her feelings. She tells Sister Maria all her fears and worries. She says why she's always so bad when she doesn't really want to be. Sister Maria listens carefully. When Lilly is finished, she looks at her with emotion. "But, my child, why didn't you tell me all of this earlier? You would have been spared so much suffering," says Sister Maria affectionately. "I didn't want to hear that I am a bad child that my parents don't like, so they don't even want to see me for Christmas," Lilly says quietly. "But, Lilly, it's not like that!" says Sister Maria in surprise. "It's not?" Lilly asks surprised now as well. "Oh, child, if only I had known it, I would have told you much earlier," says Sister Maria sadly. Lilly looks at Sister Maria. "What would you have said?" she wants to know. Sister Maria tries to find the right words. "You know, Lilly," she begins hesitantly, "your parents didn't give you away because you were trouble..." Lilly listens intently. "Your parents had a serious car accident when you were four months old.

109

Your father died at the scene of the accident immediately, and your mother died in the hospital two hours later. You were in the car, too, but you weren't injured. Nevertheless, you came to the children's hospital for observation. You came here a week later because there were no relatives who could have taken you. Your grandparents also had died, and your parents had no siblings," says Sister Maria sadly. Lilly takes three deep breaths. "I think I can't breathe," she says and jumps up. In her pajamas and barefoot, she runs out of her room. "Lilly, wait! Where do you want to go?" calls Sister Maria Lilly. But Lilly can no longer hear her. As fast as she can, she runs to Winnie's room.

Without knocking, she opens the door and throws herself on his bed. There she starts to cry loudly. Winnie, who was about to bite his second slice of bread, looks at her with wide eyes. He immediately puts the bread on the plate, runs to Lilly, and sits next to her. "What's going on, Lilly?" he asks concerned. "Did you get into trouble after all?" he wants to know. But Lilly doesn't answer. Winnie turns helplessly to Sister Maria, who has just come into the room. With a sigh, she stops in front of the bed. Winnie looks uncertainly at Lilly and then at Sister Maria. "What does she have?" he wants to know from her. "Lilly has just learned something that probably made her sad," Sister Maria tries to explain. "And what is that?" Winnie still asks. "I don't know if Lilly wants me to talk about it," Sister Maria says uncertainly. "Winnie may know. Winnie is my friend," Lilly says suddenly. "Are you sure, Lilly?" Sister Maria confirms. "Yes," Lilly replies quietly and starts crying again. "All right," says Sister Maria and tells Winnie the story. Winnie listens carefully. When Sister Maria is done, Winnie looks at Lilly and then looks back at Sister Maria. Unsure of what to say,

111

he lowers his eyes to the ground. "Would you like to talk about it?" asks Sister Maria lovingly. Winnie and Lilly don't answer. Sister Maria goes out and comes back shortly thereafter with Lilly's tray. "Maybe you'd like to eat something together," she says, placing the tray on the table next to Winnie's tray. When the two still don't answer, she looks over at them. "If you want to talk or need something, come to me." Winnie nods and looks at her sadly. Sister Maria sighs and then quietly leaves the room.

"Would you like to have a slice of bread with chocolate cream?" Winnie asks after a few minutes of silence. "I can do that quite well," he says, trying to sound cheerful. "I don't want to eat anything," Lilly replies sadly. Winnie thinks for a moment. "I'll make one for you anyway. If you're hungry later, it's done," he says, jumping off the bed. When he arrives at the table, he paints Lilly's slice of bread with the most beautiful chocolate cream

112

soccer ball he has ever seen. When he's done, he peels the two mandarins and arranges them like a big sun on the tray. He also decorates the sun with chocolate cream. Then he sits down on the armchair and looks contentedly at his work of art.

Lilly is watching Winnie closely. "What did you do there?" she asks him and wipes the thick tears from her eyes. "I made your food for you later," he says cheerfully. Lilly looks at the table. "Have you eaten anything yet?" she asks him. "Yes, I've already eaten a slice of bread," replies Winnie. "And are you still hungry?" Lilly asks. "Yes, I am. But I'll wait until you're hungry. Eating together is a lot more fun," Winnie replies confidently. Lilly sighs, then looks at the table, and then back at Winnie. "Well, I'm hungry," she says quietly, gets up, and goes to the table. When she looks at Winnie's artwork, she smiles. "You made me a soccer ball and a sun," she says. "Yes, especially for you," says Winnie cheerfully. "Thank you!" Lilly replies and sits down at the table with Winnie. Together they eat their dinner. In the meantime, they have a lot to tell each other.

After dinner, Winnie looks at Lilly and says, "You see, Lilly, I told you you weren't trouble!" Winnie and Lilly look thoughtfully but contentedly from the window.

The next morning, Winnie and Lilly are awakened by knocking on the door. Sister Maria comes in and laughs, "So, you two sleepyheads, get up! Today is a nice day!" she says and pulls open the curtains. Winnie and Lilly had secretly carried Lilly's mattress and bedding into Winnie's room that night. Sister Maria saw this but said nothing about it, although boys and girls usually have to sleep strictly separate. She has recognized that Winnie and Lilly have a close relationship and are mutually beneficial and supportive. And after what Lilly learned yesterday, it made more sense to her that Lilly is not alone at night. "Hurry up! Get ready, you little rascals, and then come washed and combed for breakfast. The others are already waiting for you." Sister Maria pulls the covers off both of them and laughs. Then she leaves the room.

Ten minutes later, Winnie and Lilly are neatly combed and dressed in the breakfast room. Lilly's gaze falls on her empty space. Also, Winnie's place setting is not there as usual.

"Where should we sit?" Lilly asks quietly. "I thought you might want to sit at the big table with us," says Sister Maria, pointing to the two free and covered seats. "Are we really allowed to sit at the table?" Lilly asks surprised. "Unless you don't want to?" asks Sister Maria. "Oh, yes, gladly," replies Lilly and looks at Winnie. "You want to, too, don't you, Winnie?" Winnie nods. "Yes, this will be fun," he says cheerfully. Winnie and Lilly take their places, and shortly afterward, everyone starts eating.

Later Lilly even helps with clearing without being asked to do so. Winnie also carries his dishes to the dishwasher and puts sausage and cheese in the fridge. When Winnie is just out of earshot, Lilly looks at Sister Maria. "Can you come to my room right now?" she asks quietly. "Of course, my child. Has something happened?" Sister Maria asks concerned. "No, no, everything's fine," replies Lilly, "It's a surprise for Winnie. But he shouldn't

116

know, ok?" Sister Maria smiles. "All right," she says and nods. When Winnie comes back in, Lilly quickly takes three jam jars and also carries them to the fridge. Winnie, who watched Lilly, quickly runs to Sister Maria.

"Sister Maria, can you come to my room?" he asks her now. "Of course, Winnie, did something happen?" asks Sister Maria. "No, no, everything's fine," replied Winnie like Lilly before, "It's a surprise for Lilly. But she shouldn't know, ok?" Sister Maria smiles again. "All right," she replies,

117

trying not to show her happiness too much so that neither of them notices anything. Winnie and Lilly use a white lie and tell each other that they are still a bit tired from yesterday and want to lie down. After carrying Lilly's mattress and bedding back to her room, they agree to meet in the late afternoon and go to their rooms.

Because Winnie's room is on the corridor first, Sister Maria decides to go to him first. After knocking, she enters the room. Winnie was waiting impatiently for her. "Oh, Sister Maria, there you are at last. I urgently need your help," he cheerfully begins. "How can I help you, little guy?" asks Sister Maria, also happy. "Listen, Santa Claus usually gives the children something for Christmas, but I thought that I would also like to give Lilly something for Christmas. I want to buy

118

her goalkeeper gloves and a new soccer book," explains Winnie excitedly. "Goalkeeper gloves and a soccer book?" Sister Maria asks. "Yes, because Lilly likes soccer so much and played soccer so well with the boys." Winnie almost overturns when he talks out of sheer excitement. Sister Maria thinks. "Would you like to explain that to me briefly? I can't follow you at all," she asks him. Winnie quickly tells her what they experienced on the soccer field. After Winnie is done, Sister Maria looks at Winnie. "I didn't know that Lilly loved soccer so much," she says in surprise, "but I want to help you. What exactly can I do?" she would like to know. "I need to know how to make money so I can buy these things for Lilly," Winnie explains. "That is very complicated. I think it's easier if I give you the money, and you buy something with it," suggests Sister Maria. But Winnie shakes his head, "No, no, I want to *earn* something myself." He thinks. "Do you think I should sing something in the city?"

"Sing?" asked Sister Maria again in surprise. Winnie fears that Sister Maria won't be able to follow him again, so he quickly tells her the story of the beggar. Sister Maria thinks. "Well, it's a possibility, but I don't think it works so easily," she says thoughtfully. "Hey, I don't sing that badly," says Winnie defiantly. Sister Maria laughs, "It wasn't meant that way," she says "I just don't think you can get so much together." Suddenly Winnie starts to smile. "Oh, I know what! I have a great idea," he calls, clapping his hands with excitement. "I have to go, Sister Maria. I'm in a hurry." With these words, he leaves Sister Maria in his room. He quickly puts on his coat and runs to the front door.

After he has closed the door behind him, he runs as fast as he can.

"This little guy," Sister Maria says quietly to herself and leaves his room to go to Lilly.

For the first time in a long time, Lilly calls her in after knocking. After Sister Maria has entered and closed the door, she goes to Lilly at the table by the window. "What are you painting there, my child?" Sister Maria asks interested. "I want to sew this here. Can you help me?"

"You? Sew?" asked Sister Maria in astonishment. "You can't stand sewing, or so you always say." "Yes, but now," replies Lilly. "Sure! And what do you want to do?" Sister Marie inquires. "Look, this is a dress and the matching hat," explains Lilly. "And so you want to give that to Winnie?" asks Sister Maria. "Exactly. That's why I want to sew flowers on it because he likes flowers so much."

Sister Maria thinks. "But you have set yourself up for a big task," she says. "Yes, that's true, but it's for Winnie. Can you please help me with this?" Lilly asks again. "All right, let's start," replies Sister Maria. "Oh, that's great, thanks!" Lilly says happily.

Lilly suddenly stops on the way to the craft room. "There is a problem." Sister Maria looks at Lilly. "We don't know what size Winnie is," Sister Maria smiles. "This is not a problem. We'll just borrowing a Winnie dress and hat while we cut the fabric," she suggests. "But what if Winnie sees it?

He's in his room because he wanted to rest a little." Sister Maria thinks, "Lilly doesn't know that Winnie left earlier to get something." "I have an idea. I will go to Winnie and tell him that I need his help briefly. You go to his room in five minutes and quickly take a dress and a hat. Then you go into the needlework room, take the large drawing paper, and put his clothes on it. You trace the outlines and then quickly bring the things back to his room. I will try to distract Winnie for ten minutes!"

"It's a great idea," says Lilly happily. "I quickly will go back to my room and stay there for five minutes. We'll meet in the craft room in about 20 minutes. Ok?"

"That's exactly how we will do it," confirms Sister Maria.

As discussed, Lilly and Sister Maria meet in the craft room just 20 minutes later. "I did it all," says Lilly happily. "Did Winnie notice anything?" she asks Sister Maria. "No, he didn't," she replies with a smile. Together they get to work.

At the same time…

"Oh, hello, Winnie. Nice to see you," greets the seller from the bakery. "Hello. I'm also happy to be here again," replies Winnie. The seller looks around. "Are you alone here?" she asks Winnie. "Yes, Lilly doesn't know I'm here. I want to give her something for Christmas, and I wanted to ask you something about it," explains Winnie. The saleswoman smiles at Winnie, "That's nice of you. How can I help you with that?"

"I want to give Lilly goalkeeper gloves and a soccer book, but I need some money for that. Sister Maria wanted to give me something, but I would rather earn it myself. I want to work for the
124

money, and so I wanted to ask you if I can help you here to make some money?" explains Winnie. "Oh, that's nice of you. But why do you want to give her goalkeeper gloves and a soccer book?" asks the shop assistant in astonishment. "That's because…" At that moment Jonas comes out of the bakery. "Winnie? What are you doing here? I mean…Is Lilly here, too? I wanted to ask." Jonas looks around the salesroom shyly. "Hello Jonas, but it's a surprise to see you here. No, Lilly is not here, and she doesn't even know I'm here," replies Winnie. "You know each other?" The saleswoman asks surprised. Just when Jonas wanted to answer, the saleswoman repeated aloud, "Goalkeeper gloves and a soccer book? Is this for the Lilly from the orphanage with whom you played soccer recently?" she asks. "Um, you could say that," Winnie replies hesitantly, grimacing. The shop assistant sees Winnie's reaction and asks uncertainly, "Did I say something wrong?" Winnie

shakes her head, "Something wrong? No."
"But?"

"Well, Lilly didn't want to tell Jonas she was from the orphanage because I think she was embarrassed," explains Winnie. "But why is she embarrassed?" Jonas asks firmly. Winnie thinks of what Lilly said to him that orphans are troublesome and nobody would like them. Winnie looks uncertainly between Jonas and the seller. "I think Lilly wouldn't like me to talk about it," he says quietly. "It's very nice of you, Winnie," replies the saleswoman. "And, to come back to your original question, I think I have a job for you that you could do," she says gently. "Oh, that would be great! What can I do?" Winnie asks enthusiastically. "Jonas was just about to sell Gingerbread Men outside at the booth. If you want, you can help him with it," suggests the shop assistant. "That sounds great," says Winnie and Jonas agrees. "Well, go ahead. There is a lot to do," says the saleswoman cheerfully. Winnie and
126

Jonas already grab the big basket, which is full of Gingerbread Men, and go outside to the stand. Shortly afterward, long lines form in front of the booth, so that Winnie and Jonas have their hands full.

After two hours, the last Gingerbread Man is sold, so the two have to get supplies.

At the same time…

"Once you know how to do it, it's not that difficult anymore," says Lilly happily and proudly holds up the self-sewn dress to examine it.

"Yes, you got it really quick," says Sister Maria. "Now the hat," says Lilly and is already in front of the fabric shelf. "I think the light green goes very well with the yellow dress. I want to make the hat light green," she says, pulling the light green fabric off the shelf. "Yes, I also like light green a lot," Sister Maria agrees. Lilly transfers the outline of the paper to the fabric. As Sister Maria showed her earlier, she draws an extra centimeter on the edge so that she can sew the fabric together nicely at this point without the hat becoming too tight. Sister Maria watches Lilly closely and is happy that Lilly is doing something with joy and of her own accord for the first time. "She must really like Winnie," she thinks, and at the same time hopes that the pain of separation will not be that bad if Winnie has to go home to Santa Claus again.

At the same time…

"I wish you a Merry Christmas," says Winnie cheerfully, handing over two carefully packed Gingerbread Men to a lady customer. "Thank you,

I wish you that, too," says the lady and says goodbye. "You can do that really well," says Jonas, while serving a gentleman. "Thanks, Jonas. It's really a lot of fun," replies Winnie. "And I'm doing it for Lilly to give her something," he adds. Jonas hesitates briefly and then asks, "Winnie, do you think Lilly will come back to play soccer?" Winnie thinks, "We have to get her to do it somehow, but how?"

"Maybe my father can help with this?" Jonas wonders. "Your father?" Winnie asks curiously. "Yes, he's the soccer coach of our team. Maybe I can talk to him. And with my mother," answers Jonas. "Does your mother play soccer, too?" Winnie wants to know. Jonas laughs, "No, she prefers to bake lots of cakes and cookies and supplies our entire soccer team with them." Winnie looks confusedly at Jonas. "I'm afraid I don't understand. Why is your mother baking so much?" Now Jonas laughs a little louder. "But, Winnie, why do you think I can help in the bakery?

I'm only ten. Children aren't allowed to work at all," explains Jonas. "Wait, does that mean that your mother is the dear saleswoman from the bakery?"

"Exactly! She is my mother," confirms Jonas. "And your father is the soccer coach of your team?" Jonas nods. "So, does your father work in the bakery, too?" Winnie asks. Jonas shakes his head, "No, my father is a banker," he replies. "Somehow it's all a very strange coincidence," says Winnie quietly. "That my father is a banker?" asks Jonas. "No," laughs Winnie, "that we were only here, met your mother, then went to the soccer field where we met you, and now it turns out that your mother owned the bakery and you are on a soccer team that your father coaches," explains Winnie. "Oh, you know, Winnie, maybe everything should happen the same way," Jonas replies. "I'm afraid I don't understand what you mean, Jonas."

"Let me do it. I have an idea there," laughs Jonas and winks at Winnie. "But you're mysterious," replies Winnie and also laughs while he sells the last Gingerbread Man from the basket to another lady.

"I'm afraid we have to get new ones," says Winnie cheerfully. "That's right, you hard-working helper," Jonas answers just as cheerfully. Together they go to the bakery with the empty basket.

At the same time...

"Perfect," says Lilly, pulling the self-sewed hat onto her head. With a beam of joy, she looks at Sister Maria. "I have to say, my child, you really did that very nicely. Winnie will certainly be very happy about it," says Sister Maria with conviction. "Yes, but something very important is missing so that Winnie can be really happy about it," Lilly replies excitedly. Sister Maria thinks. "Hmm, what's missing?"

"Well, the flowers," replies Lilly, "Colorful flowers have to be sewn on everywhere! I told you that earlier," Lilly reminds Sister Maria. "Oh, yes, you mean those like Winnie has in his room, right?" "Yes, Winnie loves colorful flowers. They definitely have to be there. Otherwise my gift is only half perfect," Lilly explains, still excited with sheer joy. "Well, then we'll sew flowers for the dress and the hat," Sister Maria agrees. "Great," Lilly replies and jumps up to walk to the shelf.

Once there, she takes out many different colors of fabric and brings them all to the table. She immediately begins to paint a beautiful large flower on the paper.

At the same time…

"Your mother was probably very surprised that we already sold the second full basket of Gingerbread Men," Winnie offers. "Yes, I think so, too," laughs Jonas, "but it really works so well with you." "It's still really a lot of fun," says Winnie. "I overheard that you want to buy goalkeeper gloves and a soccer book for Lilly." Winnie nods, "Yes, that's true. I want to give her that tomorrow evening."

"So if you want, I would be happy to go with you and help you with it," Jonas offers. "Really? Oh, that would be great!" answers Winnie and claps his hands with joy. "Yeah, sure, we'll just go out afterwards and get everything you need." "Yes, I would like that. Thank you, Jonas!" replies Winnie.

After another hour, they also sold the last

Gingerbread Man from the third basket. "I think we're finished for today, Winnie. These were the last Gingerbread Man in my mother's bakery," says Jonas and begins to clear everything up. "Time passed very quickly," says Winnie. "Especially in the last hour. We had a lot to do again," he adds. "Yes, that's right," confirms Jonas. Together they set out to go to the bakery.

"Are you back already?" Jonas mother asks in surprise. "Yes, Winnie is really a natural when it comes to selling," says Jonas. "Admit it. You all ate the treats yourself," she says, tapping Winnie on his thin stomach. Winnie has to start laughing. "Hey, I'm so ticklish," he says, stretching his stomach out as hard as he can. "Yes, look, everyone in there," he continues to laugh. Winnie has to laugh so hard that he gets a hiccup. "We really didn't eat a single one," says Jonas, handing over his mother's wallet. "Everything's in here," he says. "Well, if that's the case, then sit down

136

quickly at the table. I'll be right back," she says to the two of them and disappears into the bakery. Shortly afterwards she comes out again. "I saved these especially for you," she says, placing a Gingerbread Man and a warm cup of cocoa with cream on each table. "Now you warm up a bit and strengthen yourself a little. You definitely have something planned today, don't you?" says Jonas' mother and smiles knowingly at them. "That's right. I'm helping Winnie choose Lilly's gifts," Jonas replies. "Exactly," agrees Winnie. "I thought so," Jonas mother replies and winks at the two of them.

At the same time…

"Now we have made 32 flowers. Do you think that's enough?" Lilly asks, looking at the dress and

137

hat. "I think we did a little more," Sister Maria replies with certainty. Lilly takes the first flower and puts it on the dress. "How should we tie them up? Is it only in the middle that the flowers can move a little, or should we sew them very tight?" she asks. "I think we should only tie them in the middle so that they look nice and relaxed," suggests Sister Maria. Lilly nods. "I wanted to suggest it in exactly the same way," she replies with satisfaction. Lilly and Sister Maria are already beginning to sew the flowers onto the dress and the hat.

At the same time...

"So since you're done, your payment will come now," says Jonas' mother and sits next to the two. "Here is sixty dollars for each of you. You were so hardworking. You really earned it," she says, giving the money to the two of them.

"Oh, sooo much money!" says Winnie shyly. He considered. "I've never earned anything," he says. "Hmm, do elves actually make money?" asks Jonas. Winnie shakes his head, "No, not really!" he replies. "And how do you buy things when you need something?" Jonas wants to know. "Well, we actually get everything we need from Santa Claus. Elves don't need that much either. Just something to eat and drink. Then our clothes and what everyone needs for their hobby. You know, every elf has a hobby," explains Winnie. "What's your hobby?" Jonas mother asks interested. "I like to sing, I love painting and drawing, and I like to make flowers."

"Then you are very creative," she says. "Yes, that's right," says Winnie. He considered. "Do you think Lilly can play soccer as a hobby?" "Yes, of course, I think Lilly is a good match for soccer," Jonas says, anticipating his mother's reply. "You seem really excited about Lilly's skills. Actually, I thought you believed that girls can't play soccer," replies the mother, winking at Jonas. "Oh, well, you can change your mind sometimes. In addition, Lilly doesn't seem to be a typical girl," Jonas says shyly and turns red in the face. Jonas sees that his mother looks at him with that particular look, as if she knows that Jonas is keeping something silent. He quickly says, "I think we have to go now. We still have some work to do." Jonas rises from his chair, looks at Winnie, and asks, "Are you ready to go?" Winnie nods and jumps cheerfully from his chair.

After they have said goodbye to Jonas' mother, they have already disappeared from the door and set off for their next task.

At the same time...

"Both have become sooo beautiful. Thank you for your help, Sister Maria." Lilly looks at her finished works with satisfaction. "I find it really adorable, and I am sure that Winnie will be very happy about it," replies Sister Maria. "I'm really looking forward to giving it to him tomorrow night. Do you think he will put it on?" Lilly wonders. Sister Maria nods, "I think he would do that..."

"But? Is there something wrong with that?" Lilly

interrupts Sister Maria uncertainly. "I think we should wash, dry, and iron it beforehand."

"Oh, no, that's right! I completely forgot about that," Lilly replies, horrified. Sister Maria laughs, "Well, the whole thing has an advantage, too," she says. "Now you also will learn to wash, dry, and iron clothes." Lilly grimaces, "Very funny! And next I'll prepare the sacrament," she answers defiantly. "Ah, there is my old Lilly again. I was worried you would be gone forever," says Sister Maria, winking at Lilly. "Hmm," Lilly answers, grabs the dress and the cap, and says, "I'm going to wash now."

Sister Maria smiles satisfied and goes after Lilly.

At the same time…

"Look! How do you like them?" asks Winnie, holding a pair of green goalkeeper gloves in the air. "Yes, they are very beautiful, but is that Lilly's favorite color?" asks Jonas. "Oh, I don't know what Lilly's favorite color is," says Winnie. "Pink won't be fitting for her, will it?" "Lilly and pink? No, I don't think so either," agrees Jonas. Winnie looks at the goalkeeper gloves. "What will Lilly like most?" he asks himself. His eyes fall on a pair of blue gloves. "Tell

143

me, what color is your soccer jersey actually?" he asks Jonas. "We have a blue jersey. Why do you ask, Winnie?"

"Oh, just like that," he replies and laughs. "Now tell me," Jonas tells him and tugs at Winnie's hat. "I just imagined what Lilly would look like if she played on your team," Winnie replies cheerfully. "I've already imagined that," admits Jonas shyly. At that moment, Winnie's eye catches another pair of goalkeeper gloves. "I have it, Jonas, how do you like them?" Winnie asks excitedly and holds out a pair of yellow goalkeeper gloves to Jonas. "Hey, they're great!" Jonas agrees. "Let me try them on," he asks Winnie. Winnie hands Jonas the gloves.

"They feel very good, Winnie. You should buy them," Jonas confirms his impression. "Perfect! So we already have the gloves. Now all that's missing is the book," says Winnie. "I saw books up there. Do you know which one you want?" Jonas asks Winnie. "I know what it looks like. I broke Lilly's," says Winnie sadly. "Why did you break a book?" Jonas asks. "Lilly went to my room and broke my flowers and beach picture. I was so angry with her that I went to her room to break her book. I had touched it before, and she was angry about it. She said I shouldn't touch that. So, I knew that she really liked the book, and that's why I broke it because she was so mean to me," Winnie explains sadly. "That wasn't nice of you two," Jonas says, "but I can somehow understand you," added Jonas. Together they go to the books.

"Look, Winnie, here are the soccer books." Winnie looks at the many books. "Is the book you want here?" asks Jonas. "I haven't seen it yet,"

Winnie replies disappointedly and begins to look through the books. "Do you know what's on the front? Then I'll help you search," Jonas offers. "Yes, that's exactly what is on the front," Winnie squeals with joy and pulls the third book out of the stack. "Does that mean that you found the book?" Jonas is also happy. "Yes, that's exactly what I have," confirms Winnie. He looks at the price of the book. "The book costs twenty dollars and the gloves thirty dollars. Then I will get there exactly. I even have ten dollars left," says Winnie. "Yes, that's right." Jonas thinks. "Would you like to buy something else for yourself?" he asks Winnie. Winnie thinks. "Maybe we'll find another book about the Maldives?"

"For you?" Jonas asks irritated. "Yes," agrees Winnie. "I love the Maldives," he says cheerfully. "A girl who likes soccer, and a Christmas Elf who likes the Maldives. You two are such a funny group," laughs Jonas. "And a boy who is pulled by a girl while playing soccer," Winnie says to annoy

146

Jonas. Both look at each other and start laughing out loud. "I would say we go to the checkout now and then to the big bookstore. You will definitely find a book there about the Maldives," Jonas suggests. "That's a good idea," agrees Winnie.

After Winnie has paid for the goalkeeper gloves and the book, they go to the bookstore, which is on the side street. Once there, they are sent to the first floor, where the books about the most beautiful holiday countries and the travel guides are located. Winnie immediately notices a large book with a dream beach. "Look, Jonas. There's a book about the Maldives," says Winnie, happily clapping his hands. "Oh, yes, I can see it," Jonas agrees and takes the book off the shelf to hand it over to Winnie. "Oh, there are so many pictures in there," Winnie says delightedly and looks at them dreamily. Jonas, who sees how much Winnie likes this book, looks at him and asks, "Would you like to buy the book, Winnie?"

"How expensive is the book?" asks Winnie, looking at the back. "Oh, the book costs fifty dollars! I can't afford that," Winnie replies sadly, putting the book back. "I could give them the money, Winnie. I also got sixty dollars from my mother," Jonas suggests. "That's nice of you, Jonas, but I won't be able to pay you back. That's why it doesn't work," replies Winnie and turns to go toward the exit. "But, I am giving you the book," Jonas calls after. "You don't need to do that, Jonas, but thanks for the offer," he replies and runs down the stairs.

He waits for Jonas at the door. The two see that it has already become very dark. "Now I have to hurry up so I can be back at the orphanage on time," Winnie says. "If you want, I'll accompany you to the orphanage. Then you don't have to run alone," Jonas offers. "But then you have to go home all by yourself," replies Winnie. "Well, no problem. I would like to go with you," says Jonas and smiles at Winnie. Winnie is happy and gladly accepts Jonas' offer. Together they run to the orphanage.

They arrive after 20 minutes. "There it is," says Winnie, pointing to the large brick building. "Yes, I know that. I've cycled past it many times, but I've never seen Lilly before," says Jonas. "I don't think Lilly is out that often," Winnie says aloud. "Thank you for bringing me here, Jonas," says Winnie. "No problem. I was happy to do that. And thanks again for helping me sell. It was really fun, and time passed quickly."

"Yes, I had a lot of fun, too," agrees Winnie. "Well then, take care, Jonas. Maybe we will see each other again!" Jonas smiles, "I am sure we will see each other again," he answers and turns to go. After a few feet, he looks back again and waves, "Bye, Winnie!" Winnie waves back. "Bye," he says softly and sighs. When Jonas is out of sight, Winnie rings the bell. "Hopefully Lilly doesn't notice now that I was gone," he thinks.

"Winnie, there you are again. Nice to see you," says Sister Maria cheerfully. "Hello Sister Maria. Did Lilly notice anything?" Winnie asks quietly. "No, nothing at all," Sister Maria replies, smiling at Winnie. "That's good! Can you please come to my room with me? I want to show you something," Sister Maria asks Winnie. "Of course, gladly," she replies. Together they go to Winnie's room.

"Look! I bought that for Lilly," says Winnie proudly, showing Sister Maria the goalkeeper gloves and the book. "But how did you do it, Winnie?" asked Sister Maria in surprise. "Very easy. I was in Jonas' mother's bakery and helped him sell Gingerbread Men. When we were all sold out, Jonas' mother paid us each sixty dollars. That was our earning for the sales," says Winnie, still proud of what he did himself. "You're really a very hardworking and smart guy, Winnie," says Sister Maria. Winnie is beaming with joy. He looks at the presents. "Now I just have to wrap it up. Do you have any wrapping paper and bows for me?" asks Winnie. "Of course, as much as you want," replies Sister Maria. "I'll bring it over to you after dinner. All right?" Winnie nods. At that moment, there is a knock on the door. Winnie quickly shoves the things under his bed and takes off his coat. He just

151

manages to hang his coat over the chair when the door opens.

"Winnie? Are you there?" he hears Lilly ask. "Oh, am I interrupting?" asks Lilly when she sees Sister Maria. "No, not at all, my child. I just wanted to get Winnie and you for dinner," Sister Maria replies quickly. "Oh, I was just about to get Winnie to eat," laughs Lilly. The three of them leave Winnie's room and go to the dining room.

"Did you paint pictures again?" Lilly asks Winnie at dinner. Winnie nods, "Yes, I painted a little and read something," he replies, feeling guilty because he lied. "It's a white lie, Winnie. If you tell Lilly the truth, it's no longer a surprise," he thinks, trying to calm himself down. "What did you do?" he asks quickly to distract himself. "Oh, I heard music and also read a little," Lilly replies hesitantly. "You read?" Winnie asks surprised. "Yes, I can already read, even if it doesn't look like it," laughs Lilly and tries to distract from the topic because she, too, has a bad conscience that she didn't tell Winnie the truth. Sister Maria notices that the two feel uncomfortable and tries to help. "Tomorrow morning, after the other children have all been picked up by their extended families, I will decorate the Christmas tree. Would you two Christmas Grouches like to help me with this?"

she asks and smiles at Winnie and Lilly. "Would you like? Of course," replies Winnie. "I'm helping, too," says Lilly, smiling back. Sister Maria is happy about the change that Winnie and Lilly have gone through. "I'm very happy about that!" she says with satisfaction and bites into her salami bread. Visibly tired from the exhausting last two days and, in order not to reveal anything, Winnie and Lilly eat their evening meal in peace.

After dinner, they clear the table together. "I think I'm still very tired from yesterday. I guess I have to go to bed a little earlier today," Winnie says to Lilly, thinking of the presents he still wants to pack. "Oh, yes, I'm still very tired," Lilly pretends, thinking of the dress and hat that she still has to iron and pack. "Then we'll see you tomorrow morning, Lilly. All right?" Winnie suggests. "All right," Lilly replies and wishes Winnie good night. After Winnie and Lilly said good night, they both go to their rooms.

154

As promised, Sister Maria brings Winnie wrapping paper and bows shortly afterward.

Then she goes into the laundry room with Lilly to iron the dress and hat. Back in Lilly's room, she also brings wrapping paper and bows to pack the gifts for Winnie. Lilly also creates a Christmas card for Winnie with a sandy beach and describes it in the most beautiful script she can. Winnie also creates a Christmas card in the shape of a soccer ball for Lilly. He also writes small Christmas poems and a personal text on the white surfaces with his most beautiful handwriting.

After two and a half hours, the two are done with everything and ask Sister Maria to put the packages underneath the Christmas tree for tomorrow after they have been him decorated. Sister Maria happily accepts the orders from the two and promises to do everything exactly as agreed. Then she wishes them both a good night.

Happy and satisfied, Winnie and Lilly get ready for bed and go to sleep. Exhausted from all their efforts, their eyes close shortly afterward, and they sleep peacefully and quietly until the next morning.

At 9:30 in the morning, everyone meets in the dining room to have breakfast. "Hello, Winnie, there you are at last!" Lilly greets her elf friend. "Hello, Lilly! Did you sleep well?" Winnie and

156

Lilly greetings are equally heartfelt. "Yes, I slept very well and dreamed a lot. And you?" Winnie laughs, "I slept very well, too." "Did you also dream something, Winnie?" Lilly asks. "Yes, I dreamed of a snowball fight, of Santa Claus pulling the big sled behind him, of Hugo and Sepp and the other many elves and…" Winnie takes a short break. "I dreamed of you winning your first soccer game," he adds with bright eyes. "Oh, Winnie, it all sounds sooo nice, but you're probably not right about the last dream," says Lilly. "But why not?" Winnie asks sulkily and bites his bread with chocolate cream. "Where am I supposed to play soccer? I'm a girl," says Lilly sadly. "But, Jonas thinks it's good how you play. He asked you if you would come back," recalls Winnie. "You know, Jonas doesn't know that I'm an orphan. And if he knew it, he would find me stupid."

"You say that. I'm not convinced," replies Winnie and bites his bread again. When he notices that

Lilly is not answering him, he asks, "What were you dreaming about, Lilly?" Lilly thinks about it. "To be honest, I also dreamed of playing soccer, then of Gingerbread Men, of the homeless, how we decorate the Christmas tree, and that we bake cookies," laughs Lilly. "Oh, right, we didn't bake any cookies," says Winnie. "I've never baked cookies," says Lilly. "Whaaat? But all children do that," says Winnie in horror. "Well, baking cookies was not my cup of tea, just as little as decorating a Christmas tree or making wreaths," says Lilly quietly, looking at her cheese bread. "Unfortunately, it's too late for that now," says Winnie sadly. "Oh, who says something like that?" Sister Maria interrupts the two. "Well, it's Christmas Eve today," replies Winnie. "Yes, admittedly the Christmas cookies were already baked by this time, but who says that you can't do this yourself at Christmas?" asks Sister Maria and laughs. "We can still bake cookies?" Winnie asks and his eyes start to shine again. "Yes, why not?
158

We have time," Sister Maria replies cheerfully. "Oh, great," says Winnie happily, clapping his hands. "I'm also looking forward to it," says Lilly, somewhat shyly. Sister Maria smiles.

After they have finished breakfast, they clear the table together again. Winnie and Lilly go to Winnie's room, while Sister Maria says goodbye to the other children who are being picked up by their families. At 11.30 a.m. all the other children are gone, and Sister Maria picks up Winnie and Lilly to decorate the Christmas tree with them.

"Can we hang some bright flowers in the Christmas tree?" asks Winnie, holding up his bag of flowers. Sister Maria laughs, "It's a little unusual, but why not?" she replies. "Oh, that's great, thanks," says Winnie. "How do we hang them up?" Lilly asks and looks at Winnie, who has carefully placed a few flowers on the table. "We just pull a piece of yarn through with a needle," suggests Sister Maria. "Good idea! Can I do that?" asks Lilly, looking at Winnie. "I always mess it up, so you're welcome to do it, Lilly," Winnie replies happily. After pulling a piece of yarn through each flower and knotting it, Lilly puts the flowers back on the table. "Now we choose the balls," she suggests. "Yes. Should we put them on the table first or hang them directly in the tree?" asks Winnie. Both look uncertainly at Sister Maria. "You can choose that as you like," she says. "Then we'll hang up the balls first, then the flowers, and finally the candles," suggests Winnie. "You forgot something, Winnie," Lilly says. Winnie thinks. "What is it?" he asks. "Well, the star," laughs Lilly. "It still has to be on top." "Oh, that's right. I almost forgot that," says Winnie apologetically. "Not bad since you have me for that," Lilly laughs and the three of them hang balls, flowers, and candles in the tree.

When they are finished, they look at the beautiful golden star that has yet to be put on the top. "Who would like to put the star of yours on the top?" asks Sister Maria solemnly. "I think the daddies always do that," says Lilly sadly. "I think so, too," replied Winnie quietly. Sister Maria thinks. "What do you think? We'll make it much nicer than all the daddies around the world?" she tries to cheer up Winnie and Lilly. "But how is that supposed to work?" Winnie wants to know. Sister Maria takes the gold star out of the box. "We'll put it all on top together," she says, smiling at the two of them. "Oh, that's a nice idea," replies Winnie enthusiastically. And suddenly Lilly looks happy again. "Yes, that's very nice," she says and sighs. Sister Maria holds the gold star while Winnie and Lilly climb the ladder. When the two arrived at the top, Sister Maria held up the golden star. Winnie and Lilly carefully handle the star and the three of them put it on the top of the Christmas tree. For a moment everyone is silent and looks fascinatedly at their work. "You really did that nicely," says Sister Maria. Winnie and Lilly agree. "Well, come here, my little helpers!" Sister Maria spreads her arms and first lifts Winnie and then Lilly off the ladder. They look at the Christmas tree again before putting the rest of the things back in their places. Finally, Winnie puts his bag of flowers back in his room.

"Would you like to paint a picture with me?" he asks Lilly, who has followed him to his room. "I'd like to, but I can't paint that well," she says quietly. "Oh, it's not difficult. I'll show you how to do it," Winnie cheers Lilly. "Ok, I'll give it a try," agrees Lilly. Shortly afterward, Winnie took out all of his painting utensils.

"What do you think of painting a big picture ourselves? You in the gate on a soccer field, me on the beach and the Christmas tree we just decorated?" suggests Winnie. "That's a nice idea," Lilly says happily, and the two of them start painting a big picture.

Just when they are ready, there is a knock on the door, and Sister Maria comes in. "Oh, that's nice," she says, looking at the picture that Winnie and Lilly have just painted. "Yes, I painted Winnie with a fun flower dress and a fun flower hat on the beach," says Lilly, thinking of the gifts she made for Winnie. "And I painted Lilly in the goal on the soccer field," says Winnie and also laughs because he painted Lilly yellow goalkeeper gloves, as he bought them for her. Sister Maria sees the details that Winnie and Lilly painted. "The two of them have a lot of trouble keeping their secrets to themselves," she thinks and laughs. "I think it's really a very nice picture," she repeats. After Winnie and Lilly say thank you, Sister Maria looks at them. "What do my creative, hardworking helpers think of it if we now eat a nice piece of Christmas cake and then go to church?" she asks happily. "Ok, let's do it," agrees Lilly. "No resistance?" asks Sister Maria in surprise. "How so? Churches are beautiful," laughs Lilly and is the first to leave the room. Sister Maria looks at Winnie in confusion. Winnie shrugs his shoulders and raises his hands up smiling. "Some things just change," he says and also leaves the room.

After Winnie, Lilly, and Sister Maria have eaten their piece of Christmas cake and drunk their warm cocoa with cream, they put on their coats, scarf, hats, and gloves and make their way to church.

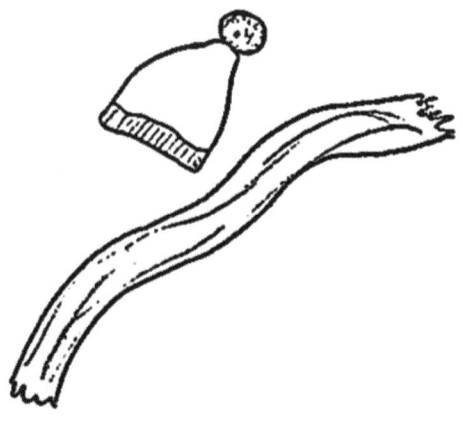

After walking a few feet, Sister Maria looks at Winnie. "Winnie, Santa Claus called earlier. He asks when you want to go home." Winnie is startled. He considered, "I should bring Lilly closer to Christmas. Lilly has changed a lot. She brought the stolen Santa Claus back, helped the homeless, decorated the Christmas tree, wants to bake cookies, and now even goes to church voluntarily. Does that mean that my work is now finished?" Winnie wonders sadly. "Winnie?" His thoughts are interrupted by Sister Maria's words. "Well, you can tell Santa that I'm still busy here, and I can't go home because of that," he replies firmly. Sister Maria laughs, "Yes, Santa Claus knows you very well. He knew you would say something like that."

"Winnie shouldn't go yet," says Lilly sadly and takes Winnie's hand. "Oh, you two," sighs Maria. "I have agreed with Santa Claus that Winnie should stay with us until January 6," she tries to comfort them. "And after that?" Lilly still asks sadly. "After that, Winnie can come to visit us on all holidays if he wants to," Sister Maria replies cheerfully. "Really?" asked Winnie and Lilly at the same time. "Yes, really," confirms Sister Maria. "Oh, Winnie, that's great," Lilly says happily, hugging Winnie exuberantly. "Yes, that's really great," says Winnie. They go to church happily ever after.

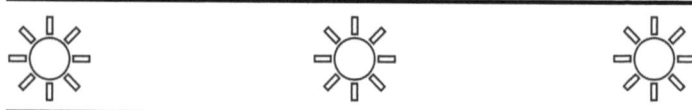

After Mass, Sister Maria talks briefly to the priest,
while Winnie and Lilly wait patiently outside the
church door. "Did you see Lilly that Jonas is over
there?" says Winnie, pointing his head in Jonas'
direction. "Oh dear, quickly away!" says Lilly
quietly. "How come? Don't you want to greet
Jonas?" Winnie asks surprised. "No, you know he
doesn't know that I'm an orphan. If he sees us
with Sister Maria, it will be immediately clear to
him," Lilly replies and pulls Winnie back to
church. "You two are still in here. I just wanted to
come to you," they hear Sister Maria saying behind
them. "Yes, it is a bit warmer here than outside,"
Lilly replies and is glad that although that is not
the reason why they came back in, this answer was
not a lie either. "You are right, my child, but we
still have to go home now," laughs Sister Maria
and opens the heavy brown door. Lilly goes out

hesitantly. When she sees that Jonas has already left, she is relieved. Together they go back to the orphanage.

"You freshen up a bit now and come for dinner, okay?!" Sister Maria says cheerfully. Winnie and Lilly agree and go to their room.

Fifteen minutes later, both appear clean and freshly dressed in the dining room and admire the festively laid table. "Wow, it looks nice," says Winnie quietly and doesn't really dare to sit in his place. "Yes, I think so, too," agrees Lilly and also stops in front of her seat. "Don't you want to eat anything?" asks Sister Maria and laughs. Without answering, Winnie and Lilly sit down at the nicely set table.

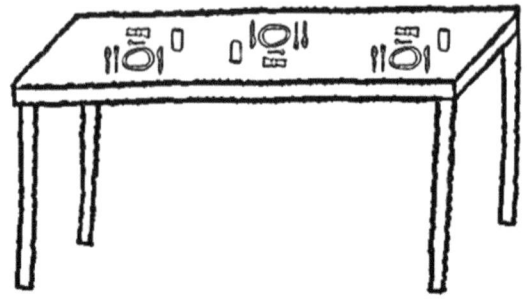

Sister Maria hands the food to Winnie and Lilly. "First of all, the starter, lady and gentleman, chicken soup with noodles and fresh oven baguette," she says. Lilly carefully unfolds her cloth napkin and places it on her lap. Winnie, who watched Lilly, does the same. Sister Maria smiles and wishes them both a good appetite. After Winnie and Lilly also have wished everyone a good appetite, they start eating. Soon they are finished with the first course.

"Let's get to the main course," says Sister Maria after putting the soup plates aside. "Next dumplings, red cabbage, and roast beef in brown sauce," she lists and places one plate in front of

Winnie and the other in front of Lilly. The last thing she does is take her plate and put it on the table in front of her. The three start to eat happily. "It tastes sooo good," enthuses Winnie, pushing a piece of lump of roast beef on his plate so that it is over covered by brown sauce. "Yes, very good," agrees Lilly, while she is cutting a piece of meat. "I think it is the first time that Lilly has said that you like something," thinks Sister Maria and smiles. "Do you like it, too?" Winnie wants to know, interrupting her thoughts. "Pardon? Yes, very good, thank you!"

"Were you just distracted?" Winnie asks in surprise. "To be honest, I was just thinking about past festivals and food," Sister Maria replies. "I was pretty angry," Lilly says quietly. "Oh, my child, you weren't angry, you were just very disappointed and hurt," says Sister Maria and sighs. "I'm sorry," Lilly apologizes, looking sadly at her plate. Winnie watches Lilly and Sister Maria in silence and instead shoves another piece of dumpling in brown sauce. "What do you think of it if we just make a fresh start?" suggests Sister Maria. "You mean we're not talking about how it was before?" Lilly asks quietly. "We only talk about it if you want and if it helps you. But we're not talking about it to make you feel bad. Being sad is okay and sometimes has to be, but feeling bad is not right in this context," says Sister Maria affectionately. "That sounds good," Lilly replies, smiling tentatively. "I think so, too," says Winnie, pushing his last piece of dumpling through the brown sauce and then making it disappear in his mouth. He carefully wipes his mouth and takes a large sip of orange juice.

"So who would like dessert?" asked Sister Maria shortly afterwards and laughed. "Phew, I'm almost full, but it would be a shame to let the dessert go to waste," Lilly laughs, too. "Well, I still have a little space in my stomach," says Winnie cheerfully, pressing against his upper abdomen. "Understood, lady and gentleman," Sister Maria
172

says cheerfully and hands Winnie and Lilly their desserts. "First, a chocolate mousse with cream with fresh fruit," she lists again and sounds like a star chef. When Winnie and Lilly see how lovingly their plates are arranged, their eyes begin to shine. Sister Maria smiles at the two and enjoys the sight. After she has placed her plate in front of her, the three start eating their dessert.

Almost ten minutes later everyone is finished and completely full and satisfied. "It was such a great feast," Winnie repeats, laying his folded napkin on the table. "Yes, really great," replies Lilly and also places her cloth napkin on the table. Two minutes later, they all clear the table together.

Suddenly they hear a little bell ringing. "What was that?" Lilly asks surprised. "That sounds like Santa Claus," replies Winnie cheerfully and runs to the window. "There, the sleigh and the reindeer," he calls excitedly, pointing to the streak of light that is moving away. Now Lilly runs to the window and doesn't believe her eyes. "There really is Santa Claus," she says in astonishment. "Well, why shouldn't Santa Claus come, too?" Winnie asks cheerfully. "Because I wasn't that nice this year," Lilly replies uncertainly. "Oh, Lilly, Santa Claus already knows who is nice and who is not," he says with a smile and puts his left hand on Lilly's shoulder.

"Well, what do you think if we take a look at what Santa has brought us?" asked Sister Maria cheerfully. "Yes, great," says Winnie happily, thinking of his gifts for Lilly, which he can finally hand over to her. "Yes, gladly," says Lilly happily, also thinking of Winnie's dress and hat. Together they go into the living room.

Winnie and Lilly stand in front of the brightly lit Christmas tree with their mouths open and their eyes shining. "It's sooo nice," says Winnie, very touched. Lilly nods. "Wouldn't you like to unwrap your gifts?" asked Sister Maria encouragingly. "Yes, gladly," says Lilly hesitantly and sits on the floor. Winnie sits next to her. "You can't open your presents from there," laughs Sister Maria, and indicates for them to go to the Christmas tree.

175

Lilly carefully takes her presents for Winnie and presents them to him. "Here, Winnie, this is for you," she says proudly. "Oh, thank you," Winnie replies, handing Lilly his presents. "And they are for you," he also says proudly. "Thank you!" says Lilly, moved. Lilly begins to unwrap the first gift.

176

"Oh, the soccer book!" Lilly rejoices and tears fill her eyes. "Open the other gift, too," Winnie says impatiently. Lilly opens the other gift. "These are goalkeeper gloves!" she is surprised to find. "Yes, maybe you'll play again sometime. Who knows?" says Winnie and winks at her. Lilly sighs. "Now you have to open your presents, too," Winnie directs. Just as carefully as Lilly, Winnie opens the first gift. "Oh, that's a hat with flowers on it," says Winnie. "Flowers like the ones I have everywhere," he adds. "Quick, the other one," says Lilly, also impatiently. Winnie opens the second gift. "A dress! With flowers!" Winnie is overjoyed. "How did you do that, Lilly?"

"Well, I probably didn't hear or read music yesterday," explains Lilly. "You did it all yourself yesterday?" Winnie asks in astonishment. "Sister Maria helped me," admits Lilly. "It's sooo nice," says Winnie, very touched. "But yesterday you weren't in your room all the time either," Lilly says, looking at her presents. "Not quite," says

177

Winnie shyly. "Yesterday I sold Gingerbread Men with the seller's son from the bakery, and thus I earned my first money. Sister Maria wanted to give me money so I could give you something, but I wanted to do it on my own," says Winnie. "You really did that for me?" asks Lilly in astonishment. "Yes," replied Winnie proudly and nodded. "That's so nice of you, Winnie, thank you!" "Do you actually recognize the goalkeeper gloves?" Winnie asks and smiles at Lilly. Lilly ponders. "Wait a minute, these are the goalkeeper gloves that you painted in the picture today!" "Exactly, and I see you painted the dress and hat here," laughs Winnie. "Yes, that's right. I had a hard time keeping it to myself, so I had to paint it," Lilly says apologetically. Winnie laughs, "I couldn't keep it to myself either," he admits. Winnie hands Lilly his Christmas card. "Here, I made this for you last night," he says. "Well, I thought you were as tired as I was," Lilly laughs and hands her Christmas card to Winnie. "Also, a

178

work from last night," she says. Both start to laugh out loud. After reading their cards, Winnie hugs Lilly to him. "Thank you, Lilly. I'm really happy!" "I have to thank you, too, Winnie. You really gave me very nice presents," she says expressively. "Wouldn't you like to see what Santa Claus brought you?" they are interrupted by Sister Maria. "Oh, yes," replied Winnie and Lilly, they went back to the Christmas tree. "Look, this is for you, Winnie," Lilly says and hands Winnie a small package. "And that's for you, Lilly," says Winnie, also handing Lilly a package. Together they open their presents. "It's a music system like I've always wanted," says Lilly happily. "Well, Santa knows that you like listening to music," laughs Sister Maria. "It seems so," agrees Lilly. She looks at Winnie. "But, Winnie, why are you crying? Isn't your gift nice?" she asks concerned and runs to him to comfort him. Sister Maria also looks worriedly at Winnie. "Is something wrong?" Lilly asks, looking at Winnie's lap where his package is.

Without saying a word, Winnie gives Lilly his Christmas card. Lilly starts reading aloud.

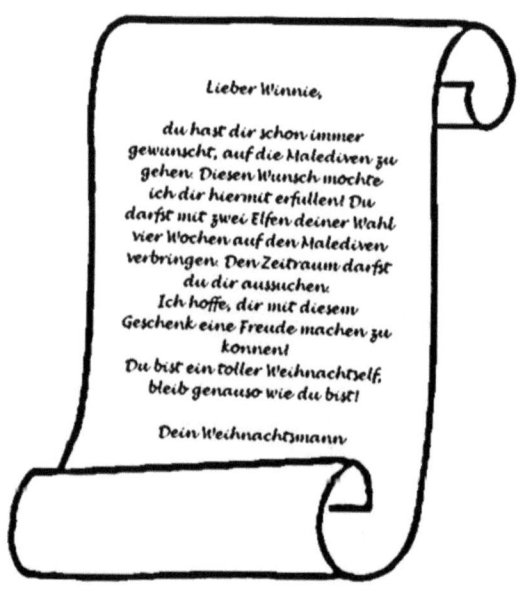

Dear Winnie,

You have always wanted to go to the Maldives. I would like to fulfill this wish! You can spend four weeks in the Maldives with two elves of your choice. You can choose the time.

I hope I can make you happy with this gift! You are a great Christmas Elf. Stay exactly as you are!

Yours,
Santa Claus

"Oh, Winnie, that's wonderful! That is exactly what you always wanted!" Lilly rejoices. Still touched by the gift, Winnie can't even utter a word. Instead, he wipes the big tears from his eyes. Lilly sits next to him and strokes his back to comfort him. "Do you already know which elves you will take with you?" Lilly asks Winnie a few minutes later. "I would like to take Sepp and Hugo with me," he says quietly. "Sepp and Hugo? What you dreamed of last night? But the two sound funny," Lilly tries to cheer Winnie up. "They are, too," agrees Winnie, smiling tentatively. "I never thought in my life that I could ever go to the Maldives," sighs Winnie. "Santa Claus obviously not only knows who is good and who is bad, but also what everyone wants from the heart," says Lilly with conviction. "You're probably right," Winnie agrees quietly.

At that moment, the bell rings outside the door. Winnie and Lilly startle. "Are we expecting visitors?" Lilly asks surprised. "Not really," says Sister Maria and leaves the living room to go to the door. Winnie and Lilly listen quietly. Shortly afterwards they hear voices that are getting closer. "Who is that?" Winnie asks quietly. "I don't know," Lilly replies just as quietly. Both look excitedly at the door of the living room. When it opens, both are startled again.

"Jonas," Winnie spots him first and jumps up to run to him. "What are you doing here?" "We wanted to visit you," Jonas' mother replies cheerfully. "Now that's a happy surprise," says

182

Winnie, hugging her. "I don't quite understand," says Lilly, irritated. "Hello, Lilly, nice to see you again," Jonas says and holds out his hand to Lilly. Still irritated, Lilly avoids Jonas' handshake. "You already know my mother, and that's my father," explains Jonas. "That's your mother?" Lilly questions. "Yes," confirms Jonas and laughs. Jonas' mother greets Lilly, "Hello, little one." "Hello," Lilly greets her, embarrassed. "Somehow Santa Claus probably made a mistake in the houses," says Jonas' father, giving Winnie and Lilly a gift each. "They're for you," he says with a wink. "For us?" Winnie asks surprised, "But we've already received our presents," he adds. "Obviously he forgot something else," laughs the father gently. "Would you like to take off your coats and sit with us?" Sister Maria offers and points to the armchairs. "It's very nice of you, but we don't want to disturb you," replies Jonas' mother. "You don't disturb us. On the contrary, you're most welcome"

"If that is the case, thank you very much!" Jonas' mother says and hands the three coats to Sister Maria. "I'll be back immediately," she replies and leaves the living room with her coats.

When she is back and everyone has taken a seat, the father looks at Winnie and Lilly. "Wouldn't you like to unwrap your presents?" he asks lovingly. "Yes, yes," Lilly replies, still surprised. Winnie and Lilly carefully open their presents. "That's the book!" says Winnie. "Which book?" Lilly asks interested. "The book about the Maldives that I saw in the bookstore. But I couldn't buy it because I ran out of money," explains Winnie. "Thank you, Jonas," says Winnie, touched. "That was Santa Claus," Jonas replies with a wink. "What did you get, Lilly?" Winnie wants to know. Lilly swallows, "These are soccer shoes and…" Lilly hesitates. "And?" Winnie asks. "Membership in the soccer club," Lilly says quietly. "But that's great, Lilly, now you can finally play soccer!" says Winnie. "But I'm a girl and an orphan, so I can't do that." "Well, Lilly, where's your self-confidence gone?" asks Sister Maria lovingly. "I think girls can play soccer, too. And orphan or not, that doesn't matter in soccer," says Jonas' father with conviction. "Even if I couldn't and didn't believe it at first, you really can, Lilly. And I would be proud to have you as a player on the team," says Jonas firmly. "Do it, Lilly," Winnie says quietly. "I don't know. Can I?" Lilly asks Sister Maria uncertainly. "But, my child, why shouldn't you be allowed? If that's what you like and you have fun, then I'm happy," replies Sister Maria. Lilly hesitates. "Come on, little one, give yourself a kick and join our team," Jonas' father encourages Lilly. Winnie keeps her fingers crossed. "Go ahead, Lilly!" he says again. Lilly sighs, "All right, I'll do it," she says shyly. "Well, that's more convincing, right?" Joan's father asks Lilly. "Yes, I'll do it," Lilly says loudly and starts laughing. "So, it is all set. Welcome to our team," says Jonas' father, holding out his hand to Lilly. Lilly returns his handshake. "I will definitely come to your first soccer game, Lilly. I promise," says Winnie. "Well, and me, too," says Sister Maria, equally pleased. "Oh, Lilly our little soccer girl," says Winnie and sighs. "And Winnie, our vacationer," says Lilly and laughs. "But, so that this is clear, I would like to have a holiday card from the Maldives," says Lilly firmly. "You got it. I promise!" Winnie answers resolutely. The six of them celebrate happily and enjoy Christmas Eve until late into the night.

Merry Christmas Wishes from Winnie & Lilly!

About the Author and Other Contributors

Daniela Landsberg

Daniela Landsberg, born on February 29, 1980 in Mainz, studied biology, German and psychology. Her first short story came while she was studying to become a teacher when she wanted to show her lecturer that Christmas doesn't always mean "perfect world" and "big family." When she was writing the short story, she found that she enjoyed writing it and decided to continue writing. When she's not writing, she likes to spend time with her cats, try to learn the piano, and get her chocolate addiction under control. As a former tournament dancer, you don't see her addiction. Daniela is an absolute night person, and as a person with Asperger's syndrome, she enjoys the peace and quiet when all other living beings are sleeping.

Dr. Rolf Peter Hampel-Landsberg, MD

Dr. Rolf Peter Hampel-Landsberg, MD, born on May 1, 1962 in Frankfurt am Main, is a specialist in cardiac and thoracic surgery. He never thought that he would illustrate a children's book. After his wife's manuscript had been ready for years and no one was found for the illustrations, she convinced him to just start drawing. What he initially thought was just a funny idea quickly became a reality. He noticed that he enjoyed drawing and painting and that it even balanced out his hectic professional life. From their start to finish, all ten drawings for the children's book were created within a very short time. After tons of drawing and painting utensils were purchased and the joy of painting developed, he and his wife decided that he would continue to illustrate his wife's books for children. In addition to this newly gained hobby, his other hobbies alongside his wife include motorcycling, dancing, playing the piano, playing board games, and watching soccer and Formula 1.